The Educational Crisis

Arieta E. Mobiley

Exposition Press of Florida   **Pompano Beach, Florida**

To my family for their
patience, love and understanding—
Paul Sr., Paul Jr. and Family
and especially our grandson,
Paul Lawrence Mobiley, III

FIRST EDITION

© 1985 by Arieta E. Mobiley

ISBN 0-682-40234-6

Printed in the United States of America

Contents

Acknowledgments

The author is sincerely grateful to all educators, associates and her family for their cooperation, inspiration and encouragement in the writing of this publication.

Preface

For many years teachers, schools and education have been the target of criticism, controversy, apprehension and disenchantment. At some times these accusations have hit the mark and at other times have overshot it.

A new society has emerged in the twentieth century having a definite impact, both positive and negative, on all sectors of the population and upon all disciplines in our midst. With a quick flip of a switch we can bring into focus a television program being produced thousands of miles away. By manipulating another dial, we may vary our environment from cold to warm or from hot to cool depending upon the outer elements and our whims and fancies. Super jets subjugate hours to minutes and stereophonic sound simulates the pitch, intensity and range heard in great music halls. In 1957 the world was astounded by the orbiting of *Sputnik,* the first earth satellite. Almost as unbelievable are man's orbiting of the earth and landing on the moon and, more recently, man's moving about untethered in space without any trace of safety lines. Travel by air and land has been altered with air transportation becoming more common; spiraling freeways circumvent the cities as they supplant much of the land travel and meander where wildernesses once lay undeveloped. Skyscrapers, affluent suburban homes and condominiums have sprung up. Huge, enclosed shopping malls wind majestically along what formerly were green cow pastures and uncultivated rolling hills. Nuclear developments cause threats of war and annihilation to hover about us.

Mores, too, have changed as ideas on illegitimacy, abortion, divorce, live-in arrangements, college dorm privileges and women's liberation have been relaxed. Embryonic changes have come about. Healthy and normal babies are produced by artificial insemination in test tubes and by human embryo transfers when conception by natural means is an impossibility.

Vast technological advancements in industry and science have modified dramatically the shape of today's world and the world to come. With this new society and mode of living have surfaced new problems. American education must be evaluated, altered and revamped to meet the needs of the now society. It is mandatory that the schools have as their ultimate goals to teach not only to be educated, but to teach students how to learn, how to adapt to the new, how to be flexible, how to make changes, how to ascertain what they are and the methods to promote the changes.

This book contains a history of education, some of the thinking in education, its philosophies, administrative and personnel functions, advances in education, some of the problems facing education and recommendations and ideas for change. This book is also a revelation and a reassertion that teachers are not the basis of society's educational problems; rather, the crux of the problem is within society itself. It must be recognized that only through the educators and the public can changes be effected to advance the cause of understanding to its fullest and to cope with the inner conflicts affecting education and our children.

Though there are many facets to education, one book could not begin to explore the whole of this field of knowledge. Here in its conciseness is a book that should be in the possession of all community members, whether or not they are parents of school-age children, that they may be aware of the workings, the intricacies and attendant problems of the nation's biggest business, that of education.

1

Today's Educational Outlook

The focus of our educational system, society's children, come and go. They are born, grow up and give or take from society the results of an educational system whose roots run deep and whose indefatigable need for change is ongoing. We wage a relentless battlecry for a back-to-the-basics approach to education—back to the three Rs, reading, 'riting and 'rithmetic. Our search is for a utopianism in education, for an all-encompassing type of learning applicable to all types of children in a pluralistic society. We are seeking an education suitable for children from the culturally advantaged to the culturally disadvantaged; for children whose ethnological lineage is as diverse as black and white are divergent. In this search, we fail to take into account, consciously or unconsciously, the myriad of influences on children today. These influences have a bearing on their attitudes, behavior, impressions and their respect for or against society in general and their peers in particular.

Varying attitudes toward adults and human beings in general, concerning what is acceptable and what is frowned upon, what is permissive and what is prohibitive, are prevalent today. What is avowed and what is disavowed in our contemporary society? What is sacred and what is sacrilegious? What is virtuous and what is impious or irreverent? Many of these attitudes emerging in the past half-century would cause our forefathers to cringe in ignominy and disbelief at the moral decadence of a supposedly advancing and ascending culture. The outlook is not all bleak, however, for the technological advancements, the high degree of specialization, the richness of diversity and the new modes of living require a flexibility in thinking, a willingness to adapt to change and an inclination to filter out the undesirable; we must respond positively and intelligently to innovations which improve or alter our way of life. Education is the pivotal force to bring about the acceptance of the responsibilities and obligations of our present-day society.

1

Past Attitudes and Practices in Education

Schools were formerly places where the teacher's words were supreme. In the 1930s and 1940s and before, each day was begun with prayer, the Pledge of Allegiance to the American flag and oftentimes with the singing of the national anthem.

In many elementary schools, the beginning teachers, into whose hands the education of young minds was entrusted, were selected with great care and discrimination. Keen scrutiny was exercised in reviewing grades from high school throughout college to consideration of their looks, dress, family background and personality. Intellectual competence and social charisma were important. Verbal and written skills were taken for granted.

One individual, usually a female supervisor, would work an entire year with two beginning teachers called cadets. She taught them the proper methods of instruction, the intricacies of exuding those charms and traits characteristic of professionals that would enhance the learning capabilities and encourage constant and appropriate development of their charges. One school district in particular stressed so carefully the development of excellent teachers as an integral part of its educational operation that it became commonplace to hear that teachers who could teach in that particular district could be successful as an instructor in any school in the nation. In this system nothing was left to chance in fostering the accelerated growth of these young minds whom these teachers nurtured. Each project, each endeavor, be it educational or social, was well planned prior to its presentation in the classroom. Lesson-planning was an essential and definitive proclivity to careful preparation and direction.

Punishment was administered when such was needed. Parents were in accord with whatever reasonable methods were employed to see that their child was learning, was obedient and was in the right direction in following the understood rules of decorum. In many cases when parents were informed of their children's misdemeanors and the teacher's need to correct the child necessitated resorting to strict but just chastisement, the parents, too, would use reinforcement methods at home. There was a feeling that repetition brings about learning in addition to the development of a healthy respect for those in charge.

Homework meted out by the teacher was not questioned or ignored, but rather was usually tackled with haste and often with the aid of parents or knowledgeable older brothers and sisters. Parents lifted quizzical brows and indicated questionable concern if no homework was given. Children, too, took the homework as seriously as did their parents who prodded them with concern for their progress and understanding.

From elementary through high school, help with assigned homework was usually possible. A knowledge of communication skills, mathematical computations and other fundamentals of learning were available. Parents knew the vocabulary for reading, many of the common rules of spelling and of addition, subtraction, multiplication and division. Unless the parents had no or little schooling would they refuse to offer assistance when needed; they often offered help when unsolicited by the child.

The impressions a good teacher made upon a student were so indelible that throughout the student's life he remembered with awe and admiration the manner in which that teacher taught. He could envision this teacher's methodic deliberation, calmness and understanding which to the student was worthy of emulation, or that instructor's penchant for literature, poetry—Macbeth, Oliver Wendell Holmes, Paul Lawrence Dunbar, Shakespeare. He could recapture the vision of the meticulously groomed and precise speech teacher, or the kind, but unrelenting, thoroughness of a social science teacher. One can often recall how a geography or a history instructor added infinite color, intangible realism and dimension to the subjects of ordinarily incongruous curriculum inclusions. For various ones of these reasons, students never ceased to be awakened with the desire to be in some particular teacher's class. Many students never fail to forego the imprint some teacher left on the students' actions and memories. The characteristics of fairness, concern, sincerity, strictness, instilling initiative and pride were these teachers' attributes. The teacher was molded into a classic figure in the professional aura of society's servants. A desire to achieve, to stand out, to be well thought of, to be respected, to conform to accepted moral standards marked an era of teacher admiration in the 40s through the 60s. The worth of a teacher during this period was valued and counted among our society's greatest assets. Advancements in science, technology, medicine, the arts, travel, recreation, and the onslaught of the use of drugs as well as social decadence of moral and human values at this time were not consuming the attention and the actions of youth. Few outside influences were diverting their attention from getting an education.

School and Family Activities

Most of the young people's activities were school related and family oriented. School competition included bag-worm-picking contests where the prize was awarded to the child bringing in the largest bag of these tree pests. Bag-worm contests not only served to prolong the life of the trees, but at the same time helped the child feel that he was rendering a service to his community and to himself. School plays, play days with all-school participation, musical programs, graduation exercises not excluded to the high schools and colleges, but also held in the lower grades, and many other programs and projects involving large numbers of the student body attracted parents, relatives and friends alike whose pride and satisfaction in the children's performances were highly and enthusiastically applauded.

Mundane activities engulfed the periphery of neighborhoods as children enjoyed the simple niceties of home and family life. Sunday school, church and related church activities, the camaraderie of neighborhood pleasures and family functions filled their time while not at school. With radio and television void during this time of today's sensationalism, life progressed at an easy and relatively safe pace. Learning may not have been instilled at a more accelerated rate, or with keener acumen or with more innovative approaches and greater specialization, but children's minds and the direction of their vision were not being obscured by distractive forces and could be concerned more closely with the ramifications of learning. Students could avail themselves of the services and dedication of teachers who enjoyed their work, who were respected for their expertise and who were called upon to be resources of help in problem-solving as well as being the nucleus for intellectual growth and cultural progress.

Athletic, clean competitive sports claimed the attention of students with more emphasis on the secondary levels, primarily in grades seven through twelve. Rivalry among schools engendered a sense of pride in one's school and fostered a consciousness for fair play and physical development. Many healthy relationships were encountered and the desire for competition among one's peers gyrated a sense of direction not only within the school confines, but also beyond the sphere of its environs. High school students were beginning to be attracted to and beckoned by many colleges and universities because of their athletic abilities in one or more competitive sports.

From the late 50s on, many schools including teachers and administrators realized the importance of communication skills. It became apparent that numerous college students' verbal skills were below where they should be, and many students were failing to pass English competency tests. In many schools of higher learning it was necessary that such tests be completed satisfactorily with a subsequent semester of work for graduation. Priorities for extensive work in written expression were given in many school systems. Lay readers in various school systems were employed to read and check student compositions. Administrators acted thusly, for with the fast-moving pace of twentieth-century explorations in outer space, jet propulsion and the press for educational opportunities for all, it became practically mandatory that schools provide the stimulus for growth in the communicative skills of oral and written expression. To make a smooth and satisfactory transition from school to school and eventually from school to career, it became clearly visible that students be guided by the schools in every conceivable way to make this adjustment.

The Importance of Communication Skills

During this time of technological advancement, however, there was a lag in the growth of the secondary English curriculum in comparison with that in other fields such as science and math. Research and studies given an impetus by the findings of intelligence ratings of soldiers during World War II and the clamor among colleges to upgrade students' communicative skills began moving with increased momentum. This is mirrored by Lloyd and Warfel, in *American English and Its Cultural Setting*, as it was stated that:

> The twentieth century has brought us much knowledge about language in general and about English in particular that has shattered centuries-long traditions and turned a brilliant new light on all the processes of language and language-learning. Research findings have tumbled over one another as individual scholars and teams of scholars have refined their methods into analytical tools of unimagined precision, and turned a cold scientific scrutiny on that mystery of the ages—the means by which men and women in human societies communicate one with another.

Further, school authorities agreed that the ability to communicate effectively is dependent, to a great extent, upon one's ability to write well, and this skill is one that comes not without effort. The consensus of opinion seemed to be that in the complexity of the many facets that stand out obsequiously and unquestionably in good writing, two are easily apparent: fluency and correctness. These two qualities often contend one with the other; the more fluent writing is, the less correct it may be.

Thus, because of the necessary propriety of good verbal and written skills to all other successful subject matter, it is little wonder that English courses are mandatory throughout one's years of schooling. We may, also, conclude that with the need for an expanded English curriculum, pace-setting advancements in exploration and modes of living, the transitional status of the English program, research in the field and the difficulty in teaching English prompted administrators to search for methods to alleviate some of the inadequacies of students languid progress in communication.

Educators throughout the nation have studied the problem of the evaluation of student composition. This problem of evaluation has perhaps existed as long as writing itself. Since the competence in schoolwork and continuous progress in all subjects is, to a great extent, dependent upon good oral and written skills, it is justly evident that special attention be given to this aspect of education. In order to communicate well, one must be able to read with clarity and understanding.

Numerous techniques of appraising written communication have been used over the years. A familiar practice was to use as a model some outstanding literary figure worthy of emulation by the student. Using a master writer to evaluate student composition has also been in use. Because master writers have been comparatively few, and those who have been willing to teach their art have been rare, their use has not been a common practice.

Another approach to evaluation, and one which has played a major role in education, is scientific evaluation, which has been in existence some years now. From its beginning, this type of rating has been objective. With mass education it has proved of little value for the reason that research sought accurate evaluations completely independent of the classroom teacher. Thus, standardized testing resulted and has been of practical value to the administration, the employer and a college entrance board. Objective research, however, has had little success in its efforts to aid the classroom teacher.

Numerous composition scales have been scientifically developed for theme evaluation in which selected specimens were used to test students' judgment on identifying good and poor writing. Results of some of these tests revealed that the tests were fitted to the students more than the students were fitted to the tests.

Today the emphasis is on more subjective methods of evaluation, rather than on the objective or impersonal evaluations. Educators agree that to learn to write, students must write often and on many subjects. Unless this writing is checked by a competent person, it is of little value in fostering the advancement of the student's written communication. Educators are all in accord, generally, that composition, essays and other written work should be graded, but the best method to use is still a matter of conjecture by many. Giving consideration to the knowledge that the English teacher's task is a most difficult one, being intensified by large classes, it is not a matter of little consequence when the question is asked: Should all compositions be graded?

Thus, the lay readers, or community former educators, used often in checking compositions have proved effective in reducing teacher load and in improving student writing. However, teachers must supervise theme writing within the class setting that students are certain to work independently as they strive to improve.

Many communities find it difficult to secure sufficient personnel to effect such a lay program, and the funds to carry on such a program are often either inadequate or unavailable. However, where such a plan is in existence noticeable improvement is seen in student compositions if the reader has checked for organization, comprehension, cohesiveness, grammatical construction and spelling. A second reading by the teacher allows for a further check of errors, reading for content and grading. There are advantages in such a program. They are: (1) saves time thus allowing more time for comments by the teacher on organization and content; (2) eases teacher checking load; (3) facilitates careful grading of mechanical errors; (4) develops student strength through the knowledge that two persons have confirmed the errors; (5) creates more incentive to write well since someone in addition to the regular teacher is checking; (6) allows an increase in accuracy since reader has more time and (7) helps to improve the caliber of the student's work.

While the advantages of such a program are many, disadvantages as well have been noted by some instructors. These include: (1) slowness of the reader's return of papers; (2) in some schools reader checks only grammatical errors and (3) incompetency of the reader. Such teacher help services are still in existence in many school districts. Teacher aides and qualified parents have their places in such programs.

Changes in the 50s

The supposition that all students must be given the opportunity to mature to their fullest capacities whether those capacities were fully developed or limited was followed in the 50s and 60s with special education classes in most schools. At this time the program was directed toward slower students. This early innovation in education gave these students the opportunity to work with others on a level similar to their own and not to be ostracized or categorized as being dull or different or made to feel inferior.

During this period, teachers continued to exhibit professionalism, continued to be respected and looked up to by society. These teachers bore a great deal of responsibility as they do today. Pressures were upon them from following a prescribed course of study to satisfying and relating to superintendents, principals, other teachers, parents and students as to the proprieties involved in conducting the classroom and presenting subject matter. Pressures, too, came from maintaining educational advancement through attendance for professional improvement in summer-school courses in colleges and universities or by enrolling in special courses during the school year. Additional demands came from parents who expressed their opinions and attitudes concerning how their children should be taught and what they should be learning; and the students themselves indicated how they felt about school in their actions, words and attitudes. They let it be known what they thought of their teachers and what they wished their school was like. These many factors, even prevalent today, increase additional taxation upon teachers and influence their teaching, their thinking, and their judgments to a great degree. Attitudes, ideas and procedures expressed and learned in preparatory professional courses and in professional settings, together with memories of the teacher's own schooldays and the actions and methods of teachers he wished to or wished not to be like, continue to be a part of the conglomerate of issues that have a bearing and influence upon that teacher's perception of classroom situations. The teacher's own beliefs, cultural background, ethnic group, social group and the region from which he has come also contribute to and affect the teacher's reactions to his students and to his methods of teaching.

The tenure of the teacher on both the elementary and the secondary levels in the early decades of the twentieth century was of long duration. Teachers remained in the field and many of them became almost an institution within themselves and an idol of emulation. In the past years and even today when classes hold reunions, many former teachers are guests and speakers. There were reasons during this period for teachers to remain in the field for long periods of time and for young people to choose teaching as a career. The young college graduate did not have an extensive array of career choices as he has today. Law, medicine, teaching, nursing, the ministry and a relatively few other choices were available. Finances, time and, as in several of these areas, being in the top portion of the class were determining factors in making career choices. Teaching was attractive at this time because teachers were looked upon with admiration and respect. The community considered the teacher one of its most influential citizens. These public servants were the caretakers of their children; they were the medium through which the characteristics of intellectual development, self-discipline, love of learning, the capacity to make sound and wise decisions and the ability to think clearly and unselfishly were developed. While teachers' salaries were low, the economy did not particularly warrant high salaries to keep pace with the cost of living. The National Education Association, while working in the teachers' behalf in the areas of teacher legislation, salaries, research, educational support, teacher rights, curriculum development and political involvement, served as a catalyst in advancing education and teacher improvements.

Teachers had not begun to speak out for teacher rights for higher salaries, work improvements and more personal job benefits. In short, teacher rights, job improvements and teacher unions, too, had not come to the fore.

Forces Contributing to Educational Problems, Dilemmas

The twentieth century is an age of dramatic change. It is an age of phenomenal technical advancement and, also, an age of dilemma, an age of inexorable social problems which are besetting not only our children, but the adult population as well. Although scientific advancement has been practically bewildering as well as unbelievable, this growth has not kept pace with ethical progress and the urgent necessity to be responsive to the needs of human beings. Influences from without and within the schools affect the attitudes, performance and effectiveness of teachers and students as well. Awareness of current trends, thoughts and new educational tools and techniques is essential if our schools are to meet the challenge of this change in improving lives, meeting human and industrial needs, stimulating economic and social progress and in the sharing of this progress with all mankind.

The early nineteenth century was marked by the dreams of new hope that our land is essentially good, but which was overshadowed by wars and depression. World War I was to make our world safe for democracy while World War II was heralded by many to have established fundamental freedoms for people everywhere. On every hand, however, we see ambiguities to these assumptions. We see chaos running rampant, fighting among nations, in cities, in families, starvation, depression, illiteracy, racial prejudice; we are surrounded by inequities, family disintegration and social unrest. This dilemma in which we find ourselves affects all of our population. The forces which will be considered are affecting both adults and children. Although we boast of many scientific advancements in our industrialized and specialized society, we find destructive chemical inventions which could disintegrate our world and demolish in an instant a lifetime of humanity and industrial social growth. The conglomerate of the entire process of technological change in our society has been greatly escalated by automation in industry. In our country today, machines supply more than 95 percent of all power for industrial work. Our work week has been reduced to forty hours and some advocate a four-day week. While modern technology has brought a better and safer life for many, it has also brought new and devastating problems. Machines are now taking the place of man and relegating him practically to an insubordinate state. Man has more leisure time and manual-free time than he has ever had.

What is the force that can secure us together, with God's help, against wars and destructive isolation and oblivion? Since our children are to be the torchbearers of tomorrow, the storekeepers of our civilization and the basis for insuring the absence of mediocrity in learning from one generation to another, it is necessary that we take an introspective survey into their training. Our most effective weapon, their education, is our best defense against wars, destruction and moral and social decay. The only way leaders can function is through effective mediation with an enlightened people. This can be done successfully only through communication and by making decisions that are amenable to the welfare of peoples of all nations.

While we hear of the inability of teachers to impart those educational concepts of knowledge that will enable students to keep step with our culture, while we hear that many teachers have failed to encourage, to motivate and to elevate the students, we must stop and ask: Why? Some say the profession is not attracting the most able and most sensitive young people in the field, and while some advocate that a return to the basics is essential, let us survey the many social pressures affecting the schools in particular and the students in general; then we can see beyond the sunset and find where the dark threats to our society lie.

Many social ills plague us today. Among these are: alcoholism, drug abuse, desegregation, the decline of the family, single-parent homes, suicidal conflicts, juvenile delinquency, low self-esteem, loose moral codes, high divorce rate, sex revolution, violence and the economic recession. Scientific factors include: space exploration, television, video, computers, missiles, world travel by jet propulsion and other scientific developments. All of these factors have a bearing upon students either directly or indirectly. These influxes in our twentieth-century society may involve and affect children, adults or both. Lewd movies showing unmarried couples in questionable positions in bed, killings, violence and unseemly exposure to all types of actions most certainly have a direct affect on our children's thinking and their actions.

Movies are no longer a drawing card unless language so smutty, so vulgar and perverse is used that the viewers would hesitate to repeat it. Sex is rampant. Illicit sexual affairs with anyone other than a person's mate is the fuel that kindles the fires of ecstasy. Ratings mean little, PG or Parental Guidance means to guide the young ones to the theater with the parents, for young children hardly able to know the birds and the bees giggle and crunch on buttered popcorn and savor the corn, language and activity about as much as their parents. The more sensational the picture, the more popular are the movies on TV and at the cinema.

Whatever affects the adults has a bearing upon the child. The use of alcohol, the most widely used and abused of all drugs, by students of whatever age has stemmed, as some believe, from seeing their parents as confirmed or social drinkers or from attempts to remain in favor with their peers. The use of alcohol is often used as a status symbol or as a depressant to overcome unhappiness and strained relations at home, dissatisfaction with one's own image or as a revelation of a disdain of society in general. Many students have been disenchanted with their family life, have become lackadaisical about their school life and have mixed emotions as to which parent they owe allegiance when faced with the divorce of their parents. Children who are seriously affected by divorce can become failures in school when before they had been honor students.

Drugs and Their Implications

Another social calamity threatens school life and adds to the moral deprivation of the students and to the teacher's already overtaxed load of educational interference. Drug traffic and its illegal use, misuse or abuse has become one of the most serious concerns on the American contemporary scene. This blight on society is found everywhere—in our schools, colleges, industry and business and is increasingly prevalent among athletes; drugs are found in affluent neighborhoods as well as in the inner city. Drug use has become a significantly problematic concern among our young people.

Although laws are in force to deter the use of some drugs, the laws do not prevent or exclude their use. Even elementary students are caught up in this web of ensnarement. Only through education, through the dissemination of information on the mind-boggling effects of drug use and through stricter laws for drug trafficking will their use be discouraged and controlled. One small segment of the rapidly changing technological period in which young people live is the exploitation and availability of drugs. A panoramic view of brightly hued pills sweep across our television screens, cover our drugstore shelves and demand our strict and undivided attention in newspaper and magazine advertisements. Fashionably dressed men and women drinking martinis on TV and in magazine ads also give young people the notion that this is the ultimate in suaveness. We have an imposing array of tablets, pills, big, little and in-between and fancy-bottled doses of medicines to induce sleep in a hurry, or to keep us awake and alert as the need arises; there are pills and potions to relieve boredom, apathy, tension, nervousness, excitability, to incite passion and to cure almost anything that ails one. There are drugs, however, that are useful if properly used and controlled. As with many scientific developments: How do we control their use? How can we educate society so the drugs may be used wisely for the benefit of man and not to his detriment?

Impressive advances have been made on their uses and effects, yet acceptable codes of ethics for their use have not been achieved. Television commercials flaunt before our youths the concept that the indiscriminate use of drugs is an acceptable solution to an array of human problems. Contemporary life has tended to magnify the traditional stresses placed upon adolescence. When many problems prove insoluble, most people down through time have depended upon over-the-counter or doctor-prescribed medication for their solution. Drugs have long been a sanction for escaping some of life's realities, so drugs are not the creation of young people, rather they are a figment of their inheritance. This dilemma of our society is one that is not unique to any particular age, class or nationality. It is a declaration of man's discontent with society. This problem is more visible in our young people but not confined to them.

We cannot point an accusing finger at parents or children alone for the presence of this malignancy in our midst. It is, however, the responsibility of the adults—parents, teachers and citizens—to enlighten the public through education on the hazards of the illegal use of drugs, and to work toward curbing its growth that our young people might not be overcome by its traumatic crush. Parents must not blame themselves and feel that warnings, threats and punishments can be the answer. Parents and children must become able to communicate with one another, to understand the things that are of significance to them and the things that need to be questioned. Parents must, with sincerity and calmness, offer information on the dangers of drug use and the legal implications involved. They must know that the possession and use of illegal drugs is punishable by law.

Many pressures with which young people must cope are too great for the less strong to resist. The ability to withstand peer pressure, family pressure, school pressure may be more than some are able to bear; this varies with one's ability to withstand emotional stress; nevertheless, under sufficient demands and pressures from without and tension within oneself, anyone can be in a position to become drug-prone.

Associations with persons using drugs and connections with bad environmental influences such as choosing questionable persons with whom to associate can be reasons for one's experimenting with drugs. Not all associations or the environment are responsible for problems our youth may have, but our young people must be made to understand that they are responsible for their own actions and for their own decisions. They must be willing to accept the consequences of their own behavior, for these acts will affect them throughout their lives.

If, however, a child must learn by experience and makes a mistake, he must not be ostracized, but made to realize that his entire life is not in jeopardy. The correction of the mistake may involve the intervention of one or both parents, and through the display of love and careful guidance the child or person may be helped. Often the use of drugs is a cry for help when peer problems are heavy; their use could be attributed to a desire for "belonging" to one's peer group, which is crucial to an individual's personal and social adjustment. Parents, teachers, school officials, law enforcement officers, employers and citizens alike must be aware of the drug problem, be able to recognize the abuse of drugs and know how to counsel. These groups or persons must be able to sense the need for help for those under the influence and, above all, to consciously and continually work toward eliminating the problem. The education of the public is a pressing exigency if we desire to prevent the results of this menace among us, for we cannot afford to injure our children physically or mentally. Drug usage results in robberies and even murders to support the habit, suicides, changes in personalities, changes in school attendance and performance, abnormal work habits, general moral decay and drug addiction. In short, drugs are harmful in altering perceptions of distance, time and space, or consciousness, and are misused to the apparent injury of the person or society. All individuals, young persons and adults, must be cognizant of the fact that every drug is harmful, even aspirin, when excess amounts are taken. When some drugs are taken in combination with other drugs, or by people hypersensitive to ordinary amounts, the results can be catastrophic.

Being able to identify the drug abusers through their unusual actions, appearance, coordination, speech and decreased physical activity is important to recognize. Many persons in entertainment and athletics, as well as other professionals, have been convicted of drug use. The media of television and newspapers transform many young idols and heroes into either questionable focus or emulation. Thus, it is becoming increasingly apparent that more stringent control and stricter laws, together with continuous education on the detrimental effects of drugs, is urgent. This acceleration is not only the duty of the teachers and school officials but of society as well.

Teenage Drinking

Michael, a clean-cut sophomore student who came from a middle-class family, had been sent to the vice-principal's office because he would fall quietly asleep practically every morning in his third-period class. He could hold a book in his hands, keep it steady and sleep what seemed to be very soundly. Had one not noticed his eyes or had the teacher not called on him to recite, he would have been considered busily engrossed in reading his text. Several teachers had reported that on occasion Michael's eyes appeared red when he entered class. On this particular morning, in addition to the red appearance of Michael's eyes, the teacher stated he could smell liquor. Michael was a relatively bright student, and his grades the past several months had dropped noticeably.

Upon being interrogated by the vice-principal who, too, seemed to detect the smell of alcohol, Michael, a convincing talker, said he'd merely taken some cough syrup for a bad cough. He offered that he had brought the bottle to school, so he could use it several times during the day. The vice-principal, upon checking the young man's locker, did find a bottle of cough syrup which seemed to have the contents almost totally filled with alcohol. When his parents were contacted, it was found that he had been associating with some older boys who would buy beer for him and other youths for they were underage. Michael contended that he did not care that much for beer, but some of his friends drank it so he didn't want to be an oddball.

Teenage drinking just as drug abuse in general is not confined today to the ghetto, but has spread to suburbia and from the big cities to the smaller towns, causing great alarm and reason for concern among all sectors of society. In spite of public school education, legal restrictions, religious teachings and public condemnation, numerous surveys on teenage drinking reveal that it is widespread. Some say the reason for this is because drinking is an adult custom and that teens are adopting the pattern set by most of the adults. It is said that adult drinkers outnumber nonadult drinkers two to one. Surveys further indicate that teenagers drink primarily beer and do so usually at home or in the home of friends, but mainly at parties. However, even with widespread publicity concerning alcohol, many teens continue its use.

In a survey at William McKinley Junior High School 259, made by Dick McLaughlin, Brooklyn alcohol coordinator, nine reasons for teenage drinking were outlined. They are: (1) curiosity—a desire by young people to experiment, (2) peer-group pressure—doing what friends and other youths their age are doing, (3) escape from everyday problems—a means of temporary escape from poor family relationships and the absence of love and affection in the family, disappointments in boy-girl relationships and adolescent adjustment in the interpersonal relationships relative to growing up, (4) mass-media saturation—television, newspapers, radio, magazines glamorize drinking, (5) availability—opportunities are available for young people to secure alcohol and places where they can drink it are also accessible, (6) lack of goals—failure of students to set goals; goals that are set, are they attainable? (7) rebellion—breakdown in parental communication causing youth to seek understanding and comfort away from the home and rejection of parents; lack of respect for parents, (8) questionable morality of the adult culture—adult habits often involve the serving of alcohol and its use is the cause of illnesses and disruption in family relations and (9) lack of communication—discussing mutual problems with children and listening to what they have to say is not done enough. In short, alcohol is used to tune in and add to the happiness generated when in the presence of other people, on special occasions and at various activities, to add what is thought to be zest to meals, for relaxation and to tune out unwanted thoughts and feelings.

Alcohol is a depressant, chemically C_2H_5OH or ethyl alcohol, medically a depressant drug that slows activity of the brain and spinal cord. It is a depressant as are barbiturates, tranquilizers and methaqualone. Some effects of alcohol are a feeling of well-being, loss of coordination, intoxication and hangover. According to authorities on the subject, alcohol is physically addictive. The depressants are physically addictive and are the most harmful to children. These drugs cause the body to develop a physical dependence. Narcotics and depressants often classed as barbiturates are the two most common addictive drugs.

Some hazards of alcohol abuse or its excessive use are the development of physical and psychological dependence; continued and long-term heavy drinking can cause eventual liver and heart damage, malnutrition and other illnesses. Being under the influence of alcohol results in slowed reflexes and disorientation, which could result in accidents. It behooves teachers and particularly physical education teachers to stress the importance of sound bodies for good health with emphasis on those things that are detrimental to one's healthy body and general well-being.

Child Abuse

In the past decade the issue of child abuse has been in the forefront of social ills affecting our nation's youth and subsequently having an effect upon our educational population. Before recent times, reports of child abuse were usually hush-hush and found in the most deprived classes. Today, however, reports of child abuse are made in middle-class and affluent neighborhoods. It has been estimated that one to two million American youths are sexually abused by their own parents or guardians, physically beaten, battered and neglected.

Child abuse is not new. Far back in ancient history children were sacrificed to the gods for a good grain harvest. Poverty-stricken families unable to care for their children sold them into slavery. In America, black children were sold into slavery and were obliged to work long and hard for a master. During the industrial era many youngsters had to work in factories to put food on the table and help make ends meet. In the early 1700s several persons were made to stand trial for the punishment of a working child and a servant who had received corporal atrocities so severely that they ultimately led to their deaths. In both instances these youngsters had been sent out as servants or apprentices.

As time passed, efforts were made to protect youths and steps were taken for their protection. Today we have laws that govern the institutions for the young; laws for children to be adopted; and laws to prevent them from growing up without schooling. Evidences of child abuse are seen in the schools. Children have been placed in foster homes because parents have abused them, for fathers having sexual relations with their daughters, for battering young babies by beatings, burning them with cigarettes and by the use of other forms of cruel treatment. Many children abducted from their homes, schools and playgrounds by deranged or emotionally upset parents have never been found and if found were dead or had been molested. Juvenile courts and social agencies are coping with many cases unearthed by teachers, counselors and school personnel.

Parents who have been discovered and handled as child abusers are usually in need of special treatment, for at the core of the abuse are problems severely affecting the parent. The treatment should be directed toward aiding the parent in getting rid of the problems, preventing further difficulties and keeping the family intact if possible while the problems are being worked through.

In 1974, the Child Abuse Prevention and Treatment Act was adopted. Its purpose: to help the states and local communities to better identify, prevent, and treat abuse and neglect.

Incest

Incest is not a new social ill in our society, rather incest was noted in ancient Egypt with Cleopatra (68–30 B.C.), queen of the Nile, who married her brother. She herself was the result of a number of incestuous royal marriages. Incest is actual intercourse between two people who are related. It is a taboo or prohibition by religion and law. It is such a taboo that it is difficult to discuss and often goes undetected because of shame or fear.

In the incest hierarchy, the most unacceptable is mother-son, then father-daughter, then brother-sister incest. Other kinships include cousins, uncles and the like. By some, incest is considered to be the universal crime, the most extreme form of deviant behavior.

Counselors, teachers and school authorities must be alert to students' desires to talk about problems that are disturbing them or are having an effect on their school performance and emotional life. Sometimes the discovery of such a problem is often incidental; at other times it is traumatic with social disapproval and legal action. If discovered within a family, however much the family members fight and bicker within the home, they still usually protect themselves from outside intervention. With or without professional help, many families are able to work through their problems.

Suicide

According to statistics suicide rates are increasing at an alarming pace among youngsters of all ages. Suicide today ranks as the third leading cause of death among teens, behind accidents and homicides. Many authorities believe suicide is the number-one killer; that a number of the accidents and homicides are actually suicides in disguise. Some call those who slowly destroy themselves with drugs and alcohol "chronic suicides." In the United States an average of eighteen teenagers a day take their lives—6,500 every year; and 1,000 attempts at suicide are made daily by children and adolescents. Suicide is a cry for help that needs to be heeded. Dr. Michael Peck, one of the nation's leading suicidologists, estimates that "somewhere in the neighborhood of a million or more children move in and out of suicidical crises."

In twenty years, statistics indicate that the suicide rate between 1955 and 1975 nearly tripled—from 4.1 per 100,000 in 1955 to 11.8 per 100,000 in 1975. The suicide rates practically doubled between 1965 and 1975. The latest statistics reveal that the rate escalated between 1974 and 1975 by 10 percent. The increase in the rate of suicides for young people is ten times the growth in the suicide rate for the population as a whole. Teen suicide as indicated increased 300 percent between 1955 and 1975; the rate for the general public rose less than 20 percent.

Among college students suicide is the second cause of death. Most high school students who attempt suicide very often have parents in mind so they can be rescued. Unlike the high school student, college students in most instances are living away from home for the first time. Many college students have contemplated suicide before they reached college. In the Josselyn Clinic's service area, which includes ten Chicago suburbs traversing a twenty-mile tract of lakefront, one of the most exclusive areas in the country, more teens become statistics than any-where else in Illinois. Ending in the summer of 1980 during a period of seventeen months, twenty-eight teenagers committed suicide, eighteen by shooting, eight by hanging and two by lying prostrate in front of trains.

Many young people in our schools OD on drugs, take an overdose of aspirin or other medicines found in their own medicine cabinets and are rushed to emergency rooms in area hospitals. Throughout most cities in America, similar patterns of suicides and attempted suicides are known. Although the rate of suicides seems high, it is relatively moderate when compared to the attempt rate. Young people complete fifty of every one hundred suicide attempts. Fortunately, this problem in our society is probably the number-one preventable health problem, because it is be-lieved by experts in the field that most people want to live; their attempt is a cry for help. It is the obligation of the parent and of the teacher and society to let children know they are loved; that someone does care about them; and someone does care about what happens to them.

Study after study reveals that 80 percent of persons committing suicide gave repeated cries for help and talked openly beforehand of committing suicide before their deaths. As many as four out of five who kill themselves have attempted at least one time before they were suc-cessful. When the initial talk fails, the cries become more dramatic. Most teens do not actually want to do away with themselves. They usually want someone to turn up to save them, desirably their parents. Suicide is an attempt not to remove themselves from the scene but to focus atten-tion on themselves or to punish their parents. Old myths about teen suicides must be cast aside. We can help our children through expressing love and understanding, permitting them to discuss their problems and by hearing them out.

More suicides among teens go unnoticed because many are covered up by parents as accidents, often to protect the family name, status and family sensitivities. Three Chicago researchers who surveyed 1,385 teens in the late 1970s and in 1980 found 20 percent feeling emotionally empty and confused most of the time; they contended that they would rather die than to go on living. Problems confronting teens involve severe perplexities involving feelings of failure, loneliness, low self-esteem, alienation, low self-regard, lack of self-confidence, and thoughts of suicide. Even little children between two and ten are committing suicide. Dr. Mohammad Shafii, a professor of psychiatry at the University of Louisville, said, "In the clinic we have seen five- or six-year-olds who have attempted suicide by hanging or jumping out of a window." These youngsters' attempts have stemmed from reprimands, parents getting divorces and feelings that they are not loved. Depression strikes both adults and children and is the most common impetus to suicide.

Figures for rates of suicides for children under ten are not reliable. Figures, however, are reliable for those in the ten- to fourteen-year-old range, where the rates have risen as rapidly as the rate for the young people in the fifteen- to 24-year-old group. Between 1968 and 1978 the rate increased by 32 percent. As we have said, depression strikes young people as well as adults. The median age of persons with depression great enough for treatment has been lowering. The statistics reveal that more than 50 percent of the patients in mental institutions in the United States are under twenty-one years of age. Dr. Nicholas Putnam, of the University of California Medical Center, speaking at the 1980 meeting of the American Academy of Pediatrics, approximated that "one in five children may be suffering from symptoms of depression, outstripping that for the middle-aged and exceeded only by the rate of depression among the elderly." Psychiatrists have found that suicidal wishes are very common among depressed children.

Parents, teachers and society must be aware of danger signals. These signals include alcohol and drug abuse, changes in eating and sleeping habits, mood changes, hostile and overly aggressive behavior, changes in personality, decline in schoolwork and poor school marks. Other danger signals are grief over the loss of a loved one through death or divorce, lack or loss of friends, impulsiveness and inability to concentrate. If any other distress signals are noted by parents, teachers or counselors, something must be done at once. Be forthright. Do not worry about putting ideas of suicide into the child's head; they are already there. If parents feel their child is contemplating suicide, ask him. If a parent cannot be specific, he can be diplomatic and ask why the child is acting in such an unusual way. No matter what method of questioning is used, it is necessary that the lines of communication be left open. The parent, teacher or counselor questioning with love and concern may help the child in opening up and discussing his problems. When parents and children cannot communicate, an outside person, a psychiatrist or the services of the community mental health clinic must be brought on the scene immediately. A family doctor can direct sources of help to families in crisis.

2

Education: Past, Present, Future

A Panacea? A Dilemma? Problems with Which to Deal

A crashing thud of splintering wood and the resonance of shattering glass echo and reecho through an otherwise quiet and vacated school building in the inner city just one hour after regular classes have been dismissed for the day. Several teachers who have remained to prepare for the next day's classes, a dozen students enthusiastically engaged in practicing cheering routines and several staff members pause abruptly then move quickly toward the source of the onslaught. As they rush toward the side door, an irate father red with fury in both face and language bolts into the outer main office in a brazen attempt to confront the principal whose office door just adjacent to the main office is closed. The principal is engaged in a conference with another parent concerning a teacher-student encounter. As rapidly as the angry and disgruntled parent moves toward the closed door, the security officer who has been in the office grapples with the man as a male counselor coming to investigate the disruption grabs the man's arms firmly as the parent struggles and blurts out slurring remarks. Police officers are called, and before their arrival the parent has calmed himself sufficiently to reveal the cause of his actions and discontent. In an emotionally pitched voice he says impulsively that he was tired of his son's being suspended time and again for no reason. He affirms that the boy is a bit mischievous, but he knows he has not caused enough trouble to warrant the predicament school authorities have charged. The principal's appearance, with his display of poise, kindness and his explanation of the problems, together with an invitation to discuss them, calmed the parent and satisfied him to the extent that he apologized for his actions. Authorities were certain the principal wanted to press charges, but this he did not.

The father was obviously not totally aware of the many times the young man of thirteen had been sent to the vice-principal's office because of disciplinary problems in the classrooms and in the halls; to his counselor to help him solve some of his problems in his schoolwork and his relationships with his teachers and other students. He was not knowledgeable of the many down slips his teachers had sent home because of failing work, poor attendance and school infractions.

One of the Special Education teachers in the area of the Educable Mentally Retarded or EMH program asks a counselor to talk with one of her seventh-graders who, it has been rumored, is pregnant and the father is thought to be a boy in her neighborhood whose name she doesn't know. The girl's mother is unaware of her daughter's predicament and when approached rambles on so unintelligibly that one wonders how she cares for the four younger children there at home. After being examined at a clinic for verification of pregnancy, the child is enrolled at the Special Service Center referred to as "Mother High" by the students. Here she is able to continue her education uninterrupted and is taught how to care for her child. Prior to attendance at the school, the mother and child make preliminary visits to the center that just what is to be done would be understood. If the student's work is acceptable here, she will be promoted to the next grade. This is dependent upon her regular school's satisfactory performance. In this particular school system these facilities for pregnant girls in junior or middle school through high school have been available for a decade and a half. Pregnant students may remain in school as long as they feel comfortable in the school setting. Some have remained almost to the time of the birth of the baby.

Prior to the 60s having babies out of wedlock was not as acceptable as it is today. Families often sent their pregnant daughters to relatives in other cities, or abortions sometimes were performed. Today, while some of the older generation maintain feelings of earlier times, it is no longer frowned upon by the younger generation but accepted without reproach or alarm. Girls usually return to school, complete their education and many of them who find parents or relatives to care for their babies continue on, complete college and make creditable achievements. Some continue to have babies out of wedlock and look to social agencies to help in their upbringing. Thus great strides have been made in recent years to help all students make satisfactory adjustments. By giving these girls an opportunity to complete their education, they do not have to depend upon society to carry out their personal responsibilities. At the same time, these girls must be taught how to protect themselves through the use of contraceptives if they must engage in sex and where to go for help; but, above all, they must be taught to set educational goals as their primary concern.

The Instrumental Music teacher visits the counselor's office after school and hands the counselor a folded piece of notepaper after explaining she was shocked to confiscate the note from one of her nicest and top students in her eighth-grade middle school class; she wondered if the counselor would speak with the student to see what was amiss. In conferring the next day with the counselor, the young lady smiled and casually commented without any hesitation whatsoever: "Oh, I meant nothing by the note. Everything between my boyfriend and me is O.K.; all the kids say that!" The counselor had just previously approached her with the note which read: "I'll call you tonight when my 'fucking' mother goes to bed, because I'm on punishment for staying away from home too long yesterday. Maybe I can get out of class some way tomorrow and meet you in the afternoon." After allowing the student to vent her feelings for not having more privileges at home and harboring feelings that her mother didn't trust her, she seemed to see with the counselor's help that even adults cannot do everything they want to do and her mother placed the restrictions on her for sound reasons, which the counselor drew out of the young lady. No further problems seemed to be forthcoming, and the teacher reported later that the student was continuing to be one of her most dependable and hardest-working students.

In another case, Alice's mother is appalled when told by the principal that her daughter is not reporting to school. A younger brother attends a nearby elementary school regularly and offered that he thought his sister was attending school each day. The children lived with their mother, who left for work before the children left for school. Attendance records revealed that the daughter reported to her first class, then left the school and returned home. A new student from out of state, the fourteen-year-old states she is not being challenged enough in her new school environment although the counselor had made several changes to classes the girl felt she could tackle, would enjoy and would move ahead in and at a faster pace. When the school authorities filed a report with the Juvenile Court, because the girl still would not come to school, the family moved to another nearby city. The teenager's new counselor called and reported an identical truancy pattern. The last word from the counselor in the new school was that they were turning her case over to the court.

Janice confides in the counselor with her concerns on marriage when she becomes an adult. She has been asked how she feels her present attitude, which has been so questionable by the majority of her teachers, could improve, thereby helping her in her work and in her relations with her teachers, her mother and with her classmates. She is helped to understand that more important than her schoolwork is her ability to get along with others; that if her attitude and relationships with others improve, so will her schoolwork. She is shown that she can grow up, have a career and even a family if such would be her choice. Her mother, who has a live-in boyfriend and is the mother of two younger children by different fathers, is at a loss to understand her child's disobedience in class and the failure of her thirteen-year-old to pursue her studies. The teen declares emphatically that she never wants a husband, she might live with someone, but will never marry because men are "not right." She added that her mother had told her about men. However, the student did improve after much counseling, redirecting her values and restructuring her ideas about life. Her negative attitudes about herself and others improved and her rapport with her teachers and classmates was significantly better.

Larry sleeps so much in his classes that learning with him is practically nonexistent. Up to the beginning of grade 10 he had been an honor student, a school leader and the type of student teachers welcome in their classes. The security officer and vice-principal sensed his unusual appearance of muscular coordination and his lethargic and unconcerned attitude and manner toward his teachers and the other students. His parents, who were later contacted, divulged that Larry is attending a special program for boys involved in drug use. The boy later acknowledged using hallucinogens, smoking marijuana and using barbiturates, pentabarbitol—yellow jackets and amobarbitol—blue devils. Larry is learning the hard way that drugs can make one sick, put you in prison, be expensive, cause dependence, cause many problems and cause death.

Erica, whose upper legs reveal raised bruises and black-and-blue marks at various times when she suits up for gym, explains that she was scratched at home by a younger sister and had fallen out of bed several times. Erica's mother, sensing that these marks might be noticed, calls the school to offer to work on special PTA committees and in other groups and brings cookies to offer to the counselor and teachers as coverups. The gym teacher, other teachers and the counselor sensed something was wrong. The principal was alerted, the child was checked by the nurse and interrogated by the social worker. The Social Rehabilitation Services worker was alerted and eventually the student was taken away from the mother and placed in a foster home.

While many of these examples of school problems sound familiar, they are only a few of the dilemmas faced by education in these contemporary times. Societal forces of this twentieth century play havoc on our educational systems, affect the attitudes, moods, habits, physical well-being, thought processes, curriculum and changes in our perceptions of right and wrong. These forces also affect changes in family relationships, bring about sexual permissiveness and a lack of respect for both youth and adults. A deluded value of human life and a perverted view of the realities of human existence are the results.

Education Center, USA

Education may well be called Medical Center or Education Center, USA, because it proves to be the mecca for students to go to be given the necessary prescriptions for learning, prescriptions that will lead them to success in life or at least to aid them in developing to their full potentials; to take them from where they are and guide them along the road to achieve. Further prescriptions at Education Center should aid students in pulling test scores up to a level commensurate with their grade levels and beyond; to prescribe doses of learning to help develop initiative, drive, creativity, and zest for living and learning. This prescriptive method of treatment must include a reasonable amount of respect for self and others including parents, teachers and those in authority; pride in themselves and their achievements; ability to live by the rules; and treat others as they would wish to be treated. In short, the school and education are the catalysts for student development; they are the Medical Center for diagnosing, prescribing and inducing well minds and healthy bodies which will act as a panacea for all learning ills, a deterrent to ignorance and damaging and crippling influences. Education Center is a constant builder to keep the student properly balanced throughout life and in a suitable position to be receptive to learning.

A hospital is staffed by many persons and so are the schools. Both have trained professionals at the helm who should be looked upon with respect, adulation, admiration and reverence, for only those who are well-qualified in the areas of body and mental well-being should be entrusted the care of our populace. Are teachers given the rightful recognition they should be given for having the responsibility to guide, direct and influence those most precious to us? Very few other people or forces administer to and affect the minds of young people as do those who see them the greater part of the day.

Are teachers' salaries commensurate with the energy, effort, dedication, time and societal expectations that affect their performance? Could their status be of lesser importance than those in business, medicine, law and industry?

A physician is entrusted with the care of our bodies. We feel he can cure our ills, that he will help us feel like new again. For this service he is remunerated much in accord with his skill and training; he is held in esteem in the community; he has our utmost confidence. We seldom question his diagnosis, for we feel he is the authority figure in his field. We pay what he expects and do not openly question his veracity in performance or remuneration. So it is with other artisans whose services we desire. We pay the expected charges for services rendered; hopefully those rendered are to our satisfaction. Each of the foregoing have set charges according to the visit, the service or the hourly rate.

Teachers, on the other hand, have only within recent years begun to receive fair pay with the help of union backing and the National Education Association. Inflation and the high cost of living have made the realization of fair salaries almost unbelievable. Can teachers, like other professionals, command and receive salaries equal to services rendered? The taxpayers can answer this interrogation, for they pay the salaries of those who serve their priceless possessions. But are they willing to pay the price, to elevate the teachers' status in the community and in the nation?

Are citizens paying their tax dollars or stinching on them, thus getting teachers not of the highest type for their children? Would you seek the services of a physician whose fee was so much less than that of most others in the same field? Would you seek the services of a lawyer of little-known repute to handle a case of intense significance to you?

We are not inferring that all teachers are not of the choice group intellectually, for many are in the top echelon of intellectual ability. But we are saying that to gain the services of the greatest number of professionals whose dedication to teaching and whose ultimate aim, regardless of monetary acquisitions, would be the wound and comprehensive promotion and push of healthful curiosity, we must be willing to make teaching as attractive, as enjoyable, as satisfying and as lucrative as various other professions.

Public Education and Teacher Salaries

Public education is a function of the state. In accepting this function the state acknowledges that the sound development of the individual and of our nation, if we are to maintain our stature among other nations, demands that education at every level of learning and in every area of discipline must be reinforced and augmented. To local authorities the states have delegated the responsibility for public elementary and secondary education; states have chartered colleges and universities. The federal government in the past twenty years has increased tremendously its support of public education. Among these are Title I of the Elementary and Secondary Education Act, which provides financial aid for low achievers in low income areas, school-lunch programs and agricultural education through the Smith-Hughes Act of 1916, which was the first major piece of legislation passed by Congress to aid public education.

The administration of the public educational programs is left primarily to the local boards of education, although it is considered a state function in each of the United States. Responsibility, then, for the entire framework of education and for its operation lies with the people as state groups rather than as local groups or a national group. It, then, is a legal fact that education is a state function. No matter what the organization of a school system, it is a state school system. Both the control and finance are by the people. The degree to which it is operated in local school districts is determined by many factors. We may say that it is a known fact that it would be impossible today to operate adequate schools locally without some visible means of support collected and distributed from a central agency. This is true primarily because there are great differences in the ability of school districts to support their schools. The powers of central agents are specified powers. One may say that they are coordinate with boards of education.

Teacher salaries are paid by the local boards from taxes levied on local citizens and amount to approximately 40 percent of the total salary. An additional 40 percent is from the state government through state sales taxes, while the balance is funded by the national government through federal income tax. These percentages are variable from year to year.

Because of questionably low salaries in some parts of our nation, teacher attraction in the field of education has been lessened. The top students no longer find teaching not only unattractive because of many stress factors but also because salaries today are not yet high enough to encourage the highest caliber of students into a field which should be beckoning the best minds in order to build worthwhile young men, women and productive adults. Top students in most areas generally have gone into medicine, engineering, law and business.

If public education is to serve the masses to the fullest extent and to be most effective, there must be a concerted effort by colleges, universities and citizens alike to attract and hold some of the most competent students. There must be more and better teachers and a push for greater enrollment in teacher colleges and a stepped-up teacher preparatory offering of courses.

On the need for more public support for schools the *U.S. News & World Report* (September 19, 1983) states:

> Although 3 out of 4 voters in the U.S. have no children in school, signs indicate the public may be more willing to support education. Thirty-nine percent of this year's Gallup Poll respondents said they would be willing to raise taxes to improve their local schools, up from a low of 30 percent just two years ago.

Still, money remains a problem in many districts. While Michigan voters approved a record 95 percent of millage renewals in June, 1983, they rejected three out of four requests for additional funds.

The same article noted that in a recent state-by-state analysis of teaching released in August of the same year, "teachers' salaries, as a percentage of all money spent on public schools, slipped from 49 percent in 1973 to 41 percent this year."

Many states are raising teacher salaries, and many businesses in some areas are funding projects to aid in improving curriculums by placing in some schools new computer classes, and some have promised jobs and training for high school graduates if there is a notable improvement in attendance and achievement.

Authorized by law, a school district is an operating unit with delegated powers by the state and whose actions are conditioned by and dependent upon processes, services and regulatory machinery or operations and services from other governmental agencies. Local powers of school boards are shared by law among the voters, the school board, the superintendent, the teachers, the pupils and the parents and is usually elected by the people in the district.

To fully understand the workings of school boards, a community must be aware of some facets of its operation and power since it bears either directly or indirectly upon their voice and money. School boards have specific powers which are relatively broad. They have the power to levy specific taxes, the power to determine the scope of the school program, the power to determine the curriculum and the power to establish the rules and regulations for the operation of the schools. In a state or in a given class of school districts these powers delegated to the boards of education may be subject to specific restrictions or extensions, as a result of city charter or special legislation. These restrictions or extensions, however, are rare, for most legislatures are not in accord with special legislation and educational provisions in city charters and are not recognized by the courts in most states. To define the boundaries and limits of school districts is sometimes difficult, for such legislation pertinent to given classes of school districts is not always comprehensively contained but may be scattered throughout the statutes. Perhaps we could say that the interpretation of the law is essentially left up to local authorities, their own public employees and the courts.

Parents, as well as citizens with children, should be aware of the obligations of a board of education to its constituency, to the people who elect them and who depend upon them to determine the direction of education within that district that it may have as its top priority the interests of the students and its comparison with effective educational methods and policies throughout the nation. The school boards' policies and functions must be democratic. It is the duty of the board of education to be answerable to the public and to the public's influence. Board members should be chosen for their integrity and sagaciousness in the role education must play in a democratic society and in a world whose dimensions have grown far beyond the dreams of our forefathers. They must realize that they are guardians of the state; and the representatives of the people; and the keepers of our youth. This prestigious body empowered with the duty of acting for all of us generally must be large enough to provide balanced judgment and ideas; and small enough to work effectively in meeting the needs of all segments of a community, namely those deprived, middle class, and upper class and the ethnic groups as well. This board must represent the people directly as an agency of the municipal government, yet be discriminating enough to separate educational issues from issues of municipal government. Members must have stability and strength to handle the far-reaching and long-term range of education in order that the board not be overthrown as it works to perform the best service the community has entrusted in it.

Discipline

Another shadow on our panorama of ills that has a distinct bearing on our schools and children—an ill that plagues our teachers and adds to the stress of their job—is discipline. Problems with discipline have arisen so dramatically today that many schools have security officers on duty throughout each school day for the protection of both students and teachers from disruptive influences within the school and outside intrusions. In many schools there are also two assistant principals, whose primary responsibilities are to take care of the discipline problems. These school agents have the authority to suspend students for a period of time whereby a hearing is set which includes the parents. Following a certain period of time, students are generally permitted to reenter school according to the severity of the problem, and the assistant principal and the principal have the authority to expel them for an entire semester if their offenses have proved crucial enough. Reasons for suspension and expulsion run the gamut from insubordination to teachers to possession of illegal substances; from the use of profane language to the possession of firearms.

U.S. News & World Report (September 19, 1983) further states:

> For the 14th time in 15 years, discipline ranks as the top problem in the nation's public schools, according to the latest Gallup Poll on education.
> Twenty-five percent of the 1,540 adults polled in the annual survey appearing in the September, 1983, issue of *Phi Delta Kappan* magazine listed lack of discipline as the leading problem, followed by use of drugs, 18 percent; poor curriculum and standards, 14 percent, and lack of proper financial support, 13 percent.
> Most Americans do not blame schools for the discipline problem. Seventy-two percent cited lack of discipline at home as the chief cause, followed by 54 percent citing a lack of respect for law and authority, and 42 percent naming improperly trained teachers.

Emerging in the twentieth century is a new approach to child discipline. Heretofore, the purpose of the teacher was to impart knowledge, to communicate with the child, to teach, and the child, in turn, was to do the learning, to absorb the knowledge. If the child failed to do this, learning could not take place. However, during this autocratic period, parental pressure and other outside pressures would aid in encouraging the student and would give him the added "push" to apply himself, thus some progress and knowledge were forthcoming.

Family problems have arisen with the numerous outside influences such as television, stepped-up sports activities, internal influences, the breakdown of family relations and a dearth in moral training. with many mothers working outside the homes and the wide incidence of single-parent families, there is limited time for proper parenting which aids children in being taught proper attitudes of behavior and respect for themselves and others.

Because of these reasons and others mentioned previously, the autocratic method of teaching is no longer effective, and it does not bring about the results intended. Many children fail to study, are unconcerned about the material being presented, no matter how unique the presentation, and many fail to bring in assigned homework even when it has a bearing on their grade. To be effective the teacher must know far more than the subject matter. Good teaching methods will augment a teacher's ability to impart knowledge, but it will not overcome a child's antagonistic attitude toward learning unless the teacher knows something about motivating children and something of the procedures to use in getting him to want to learn.

There are drastic changes in education today. These changes reflect a democratic trend in interpersonal relations. We no longer can make children, or adults for that matter, perform; the inferiority of children to adults is fading away, the supreme power of whites over other races and the superiority of men over women are no longer traditional. Democratic application of child guidance principles must be applied. Adults can no longer feel superior to children, no longer can they or society make children or adults perform except where they overstep their bounds and interfere with the rights of others or infringe upon the rights of others and the law must intervene. The emergence of these democratic methods of dealing with children does not negate the fact that age and experience bring about wisdom that only time, maturity and living can generate. With students today, stimulation from within must replace outside pressures which have lost their effectiveness. Corporal punishment is illegal in most school systems and only in some is it permissible only with the written consent of the parents.

New methods must be found to replace traditional ones. To bring about satisfactory results in a democratic setting, new methods must be found that include a combination of freedom and order. Thus, the teacher is confronted on all sides as she deals with a new generation of aggressively independent youth rebelling against adults and the attacks of parents and the community who are fearful of losing control. Pressures, too, come from many school authorities who cling to traditional methods of control.

Bruce Cooperstein and Art Pearl, of Knight Ridder Newspapers, in a syndicated article in the *Kansas City Times,* September 19, 1983, wrote:

> Our schools are in trouble because we expect too little of them, and that is why we underpay our teachers and the academically able look elsewhere for careers.
>
> The goals we establish for education must be concrete. To be effective, the school's mission must be related symbiotically to a society's mission. It is in society, not the schools, where our real troubles lie: We are a society adrift, unable to reconcile our contradictory world views.
>
> In a simpler time, before, as John Kenneth Galbraith put it, we entered the age of uncertainty, students could embrace the world view of their parents and teachers, and to expect to be prepared for adult life. There is no such view today. Students no longer give themselves to authorities. They are unlikely to pledge allegiances blindly or completely. They have become cynics and worse.
>
> Teachers are not the only ones who suffer from their lack of respect; parents feel it, too, and so do elected officials. Students' rediscovery of careers should be greeted with concern, not enthusiasm, for it is an extension of "me-ism" motivated by fear of unemployment. That fear is well founded.

When a child continuously misbehaves there is usually an underlying cause. Is he having problems at home with his parents or other siblings in the family? Are the problems personal, within himself? Is he having difficulty in his relations with his teachers or classmates? Is there a personality clash with the teacher? Is he in a class that is too difficult for him, or is he in a course that is not challenging him sufficiently? Is the problem a combination of causes? Parents may be contacted if the trouble is in the home and, perhaps, a change for the better may become noticeable. If it is psychological, the school counselor may be conferred with, who in turn may refer the child to the school psychologist for testing, or he may, along with his parents, be referred to the mental health facilities where both he and his parents may have weekly counseling sessions or group therapy, which may be helpful.

One example of a problem stemming from the home was that of Larry, a sixth-grade middle school youngster who walked with the aid of a crutch and was enrolled in an EMH class, Educable Mentally Retarded, a class for students whose work was at a slower pace and had to be more carefully structured. A pale, listless-looking child, Larry was a victim of muscular dystrophy. Because of his inability to climb steps easily, he was scheduled to remain in the library, which was located on the first floor, for two periods. One period was his homeroom and the other was, more or less, an emergency or special study period in which he used the time to prepare lessons for one class. He constantly annoyed the other children in the library, asked numerous questions of the librarian, blurting them out often without provocation, and wanted to move about constantly, which did not add to the quietness of a supposedly quiet area. His EMH teacher also had problems with him. He was constantly fidgeting and doing things to attract the attention of the other children. It was discovered later that the child had seen his father dangling from a rope after having hanged himself, and a year later the child was jubilant because he had a new red-headed baby brother. The mother was not married to the father, who was in prison and, perhaps, had not seen the child recently if ever.

Larry's problems, just as those of many other children, are deep-seated. A social worker visited Larry's home and counseling services were made available to him. Some improvement was seen; he became somewhat more independent and self-reliant.

Guidance and direction are needed by children of all age groups beyond what the classroom teacher is capable of providing, for at best her job is multifaceted. The teacher must be a mediator, a soothsayer, a diplomat, a counselor, a doctor, a lawyer, a nurse and even, at times, a fill-in parent. Counselors have become an integral part of schools; they work with children, teachers, parents and school specialists to aid students to adjust socially and academically to their environment. It is the counselor's job to confer with teachers concerning students, to study the students' cumulative records, contact parents and interview the students themselves in order to determine those in need of clinical help and refer them to the proper agencies. Through a series of interviews or conferences the others can be dealt with effectively. Oftentimes there are not enough counselors on the staff of secondary schools to get to understand the needs and motivations of all the students. There is not enough time. It is helpful to a teacher to understand the factors and influences upon the adjustment and development of young people, for it is the counselor who is in a strategic position to aid teachers in enabling their students to develop to their capacities even at times when they are making acceptable grades and are not troublemakers.

School psychologists, specialists assigned to work with students having severe emotional problems socially and academically, and social workers are hired to aid those children who have adjustment problems in their interaction with teachers and other children in the classroom and, also, in their homes. All of these persons, in addition to outside individuals such as friends, relatives, ministers and other concerned persons, may influence the child and be instrumental in helping him to adjust.

The teacher is in the most pivotal position to be of great help, for in elementary or the formative years of his schooling she is with him the greater part of the day. Although the teacher in secondary schools is with the student a shorter period of time, he or she has the opportunity to solicit the help of the entire group in the improvement, adjustment and acceptance of each individual.

One of the basic needs of all human beings, adults as well as children, is the need to belong, to be part of a group. The ability to feel that one has a place and is able to play an important role in life is essential to all humans, and the degree and extent to which he feels he belongs is dependent upon his individual social interests and the group's acceptance of him as a person. To incorporate a feeling of belonging, there must be a healthy feeling of respect for oneself and for others in peer relationships. Parents who venture too far in the realm of democracy and freedom lose their own self-respect and pamper their children in the process. In other words, parents spoil the children and permit them to disrupt family organization and decorum by permitting the children to impose their wills upon them. By overindulging the child with material acquisitions, being overly protective and forever attempting to circumvent failures and the realities of life, the parent places the child in a position of inability to cope with the vicissitudes and frustration of life when they confront him. Thus, in school the child displays a sense of doubt in his own confidence, abilities and in himself. The opportunity to experience his own strengths and abilities is denied him, and he cannot develop self-confidence in his own intelligence and his own sense of responsibility. Parents and teachers alike often reveal this lack of confidence in the student.

Parents of students who give trouble in school to the extent they have to be contacted often offer the excuse: "She does the same thing at home; I can't do anything with her." Many parents feel it is the duty of the teacher to do everything for their child with the exception of clothing and feeding him. Some parents feel that feeding them is the school's duty also, because for many students the free lunches provided by the schools are the best and sometimes the only substantial meals they have during the day.

Even with the disintegration of the family, it is yet the most important source in helping the child to feel good about himself, and it is in this setting that his religion, moral, ethical and cultural values are formulated and nurtured. His behavior, acceptable or unacceptable, is the result of this environment, the result of the parents response to his actions. However, outside influences, as alluded to before and which this book deals with, can affect, alter and even change a child's behavior. Parents often lament: Where did I go wrong? What did I fail to do that I should have done? They have guilt feelings about the actions of their children—actions contrary to those they tried, many assiduously, to instill in them. In today's society parenting is difficult. The development of a freer and more democratic social structure precludes past rewards and penalties, threats and bribes used by those in charge of young people be they parents or teachers. The democratic society places each individual as equal to others. This equality requires respect and acceptance of others and of oneself. This concept is difficult because of its relative newness in our society.

Many researchers feel that the increase in juvenile delinquency is attributable to the failure of parents to accept their moral responsibilities of establishing the proper attitudes and providing the type of environment and the kind of influences that affect the child's development and healthy social adjustment. Researchers also believe that a decline in religion in our society accounts for much of the juvenile delinquency. Our children have no basis on which to compare present-day conduct, which church affiliation and religious activities and encounters can give. Many children relate that they do not attend Sunday school, church, or have any church connections whatsoever. They contend that nobody in their home goes to any religious service of any type. Therefore, since prayers in the schools have been abandoned many children are not encouraged in any religious way to seek help in times of need, to have a source of stability to which they may turn or to learn those tenets of rightful living that such institutions can provide. Researchers' study into the contributing factors of juvenile delinquency point to the breakdown in family relationships, the high divorce rate, permissive living, crime on television (which may have an effect on impressionable young minds) and drugs. Since the governmental function was instituted of free universal and compulsory education, some parents feel that the responsibility for educating children is somebody else's responsibility, and many parents complain to teachers about their children's manners, habits and language. Teachers should, according to some parents, give both moral and academic training.

While the preschooler functions primarily within the realm of his own family, relatives and neighbors, when he enters school he attempts

to find his place among children of various races and religious, economic, cultural, social and ethnic backgrounds. Thus begins his association with his peers and the beginning of social living and societal
adjustment. As the child grows, many conflicts arise. His parents still
consider him their child; there are changes in physical development, and
his association with the opposite sex all have a bearing upon his attitudes
and feelings. It is believed by some authorities that juvenile delinquency
has its roots in the antagonism existing today between adults and youths.
At the same time that all of these changes are taking place, the youth is
attempting to be accepted by his peers, and he is usually being criticized
by his parents and circumvented in his actions by them. Their ideas to
him are ancient or old-fashioned, from the "olden days" and strictly
outmoded.

In the classrooms, teachers are expected to handle their own problems. These problems can be complex with students coming to them with
the myriad of growing-up influences that are upon them.

While our focus has been on the plight of many troubled youths in the
areas of discipline and juvenile delinquency, we would be biased in our
opinions and unfair in our judgments to say that most of our youth of
today have problems. While many such problems do exist and many
methods of helping these young people adjust and cope have been
formulated, the majority of our youth are law-abiding citizens who strive
to work assiduously to improve themselves and to reach their potentials.
They, too, have problems of adjustment, but they are capable of dealing
with them normally and successfully.

What Is the Answer?

It is believed that if the teacher's planning is thorough, if the work is
made interesting and highly challenging, few problems will occur. However, with the most thorough planning, the use of the most sophisticated
methods of teaching and the employment of the keenest and most attractive motivational techniques and procedures, some behavior problems
arise—a fight, name-calling or the allegation that "he was talking about
my mother" or the like, bringing about class disruption and intervention
in the continuance of successful classroom instruction. Principal's and
vice-principal's jobs can be difficult, and on many occasions these
school leaders are forced to make decisions that often seem unjustified
to the child, the teacher or the parent. Measures have been taken in most
school systems to deal with problems arising in the schools today. Stringent security measures and adjustment services are being used to help
solve some of the more severe disciplinal problems. In-school suspension

programs are instituted in many schools to attempt to keep students in school, to keep them off the streets and to help them in accepting their responsibilities for their actions. With continued vigilance by school authorities as to student needs and increased educational instruction of youths, seminars and meetings of revived PTA groups and school activities, even more progress in student self-discipline can be achieved. Much progress has been made in guidance and psychological services, improved curriculums, smaller classes and the dedicated services of conscientious teachers who do not have monetary gains in mind in their jobs, but who find untold satisfaction in knowing they are helping those in need of their services.

Parents must assume some responsibility to attend meetings and school functions to discover firsthand just what their children are doing. Some schools no longer have parent-teacher meetings, and the meetings that schools do have turn out to be primarily teachers' meetings, for teachers are almost exclusively the only ones present. Some parents do not have the time or do not take the time to attend; some feel their clothing is inadequate; some have no baby-sitters; some can't miss their favorite television program; others are too fatigued following a day's work to make ends meet. Whatever the reason for nonattendance, PTAs do not have the efficacy and thrust they once had. Outside influences, too, have had a severe effect on their functioning. In some areas, PTAs have become PTSAs, Parent Teacher Student Associations in which students have an opportunity to be heard. Only in elementary schools while children are yet small do the parents turn out in acceptable numbers.

Alleviating Separate but Equal Schools

Prior to 1954, when the Supreme Court decreed segregation of schools to be illegal because of race or ethnic background, a black teacher enrolled in a summer school workshop on Human Relations in the Classroom stated that the only way blacks would be accepted in this society would be when all people became the same color through intermarriage. With the subsequent tensions arising later, it could be said that the assertion could cause much thought, for there has been a social revolution with desegregation, integration, white flight and busing, not to mention discrimination cases and frustration that have had a resounding effect on blacks and whites alike.

The Supreme Court's decision in *Brown vs. the Board of Education of Topeka* in 1954 ruled segregation in schools illegal, de facto or déjà vu; students were in fact in separate schools and by law it was illegal. This decision denounced *Plesy vs. Ferguson,* which ruled that separate but equal schools were legal. This proved to be a monumental pronouncement that implied no anticipation of the future implications of the acquisition of racial equality and the fight of a downtrodden race to rise above centuries of inequity and harshness to see the sunrise of human dignity and the extension of unmitigated respect.

It was the Supreme Court that sanctioned first "separate but equal" in public transportation in its decision of *Plesy vs. Ferguson* in 1896, which sustained a law which required equal facilities as well as separate ones. Equal became a farce, a hollow word, empty and meaningless, merely adding to the desecration and injustices of an already oppressed race and irrelevant as far as blacks were concerned. Signs of inequality "For Whites Only" shouted out and obliterated any feelings of humaneness if any could come about. They were everywhere lest the black man forget—in the lofts of the theaters, at drinking fountains, in restaurants and waiting rooms. The case of Plesy insisted that state legislatures should handle their own race problems.

The Supreme Court's demise of the "separate but equal" affirmation of a group's rights came in our own public education. Brown's ultimate faith in education was simple in its terminology but significant in its social implications for change. Little did its approbationary constituency envision the soul-searching power it would have on a society of people whose founding fathers had said in effect "that all men are created equal."

Together with the 1964 Civil Rights Act, making discrimination illegal in all public places, and the 1954 decision, we may say that these decrees have been the most explosive and revolutionary Supreme Court decisions of this generation. Upon the predication of these documents has rested many decisions, questions and changes.

Today, education is perhaps the most important function of state and local governments. Compulsory school attendance laws and the great expenditures for education both demonstrate our recognition of the importance of education to our democratic society. It is required in the performance of our most basic public responsibilities, even service in the armed forces. It is the very foundation of good citizenship. Today, it is a principal instrument in awakening the child to cultural values, in preparing him for later professional training and in helping him to adjust normally to his new environment. In these days, it is doubtful that any child may reasonably be expected to succeed in life if he is denied the opportunity of an education. Such an opportunity, where the state has undertaken to provide it, is a right which must be made available to all on equal terms (347 U.S. 483, 493: 1954).

Before the desegregation of schools in 1954 became legal and the Civil Rights Act of 1964 was enacted, blacks were denied many privileges and rights that others took for granted. The blacks spent considerable money in downtown stores in many cities, yet were forced to stand at dime-store lunch counters to buy a sandwich or go hungry until they could get to a black restaurant five miles away, for there were none downtown, or wait until they got home. A group of young women from Kansas City, Kansas, and Kansas City, Missouri, prominent in civic affairs and among them businesswomen, teachers and nurses and belonging to a social group known as the Twin Citian Club, decided they were being treated unfairly by these entrepreneurs. They felt their rights were being denied, yet they had accounts at the stores and made a remarkable upsurge in downtown business, so in 1958 at the suggestion of one of its members, Mrs. Gladys Twine Prince, now of Los Angeles, California, they began picketing the stores. Other community organizations, clubs, churches and their ministers heeded the cry, picked up the torch and battlecry of injustice and thus was born the CCSA, the Community Committee for Social Action, with Ruth Kerford, another member, as its first president. This marked the beginning of the Civil Rights Movement in Kansas City; five years later such movements were prevalent throughout the nation. As a result of this fearless and aggressive crusade begun by the Twin Citian Club, legislation was ultimately brought about which gave civil rights to blacks. Prior to the Civil Rights Act of 1964, blacks were not permitted to live where they chose or to stay in hotels other than those owned by blacks. Not until this action was taken were these discriminatory practices and those in housing and public accommodations made illegal.

Even though thirty-one years have passed since the segregation of schools was ruled illegal, some schools are not yet totally desegregated but are in the process. To the states and local school authorities is mandated the methods used to bring this about. Segregation existed prior to the Supreme Court decision in southern states and border states by custom and tradition. Kansas City, Kansas, was the only city in that state where segregation was by law and this began in 1904 following a fight between a white youth and a black one in a park in the city. The white youth was killed. In some cities segregation was by boundaries, i.e., children who lived in all-black neighborhoods attended all-black schools. Several years following the 1954 Supreme Court decision that segregation was illegal, citizens in the city of Kansas City, Kansas, filed suit because they felt integration was not moving along efficaciously and swiftly enough. Government attorneys from the United States Justice Department talked with various teachers of long standing and asked such questions:

Question: Did you ever ask to teach in a school other than in one with all black students?

Answer: No, because it had been an accepted fact that as long as could be remembered the elementary, junior and senior high schools were segregated—black students, black teachers only.

Question: Did you say that faculties were all black in the segregated schools?
Answer: Yes, I did. Black students attended all-black schools with all black teachers and the schools for whites had all-white teachers. No athletic competition was engaged in between schools with all-white students and schools with all-black students.

Question: Did anyone that you know ever ask to teach in an all-white school?
Answer: No, not that anyone is aware. The tradition of segregation has been so imbued in this city that the blacks did not fathom the idea of teaching in white schools. There were such outstanding supervisors, principals and teachers who remained for years on the job and continuously provided excellent training, directing and endless encouragement to their students that the black teachers were proud of their heritage and the community valued them and considered them tops in their respective fields. They were examples of courage and dedication to the blacks and to the community in general. These teachers went the extra mile in providing dedicated, competent and superior direction to the black youth of the city. It was felt that no teachers could compare with the caliber of black teachers at that time.

These government attorneys interrogated many black teachers. Because of their reported veracity and competence, they felt these teachers would answer their queries honestly and fearlessly. From these segregated schools have emerged many students of the greatest magnitude of whom the community has been justly proud. Many are physicians, judges, attorneys, businessmen and businesswomen, government leaders and employees, corporate heads, ministers, teachers, social workers, writers, scientists, accountants, college presidents, college professors, police personnel, military personnel and successful homemakers. Others have gone into other areas too numerous to name.

The Declaration of Independence was drafted by Thomas Jefferson and adopted by the Continental Congress on July 4, 1776. The founding fathers' goal to guard the rights of individuals and to insure the development of those rights stated:

We hold these truths to be self-evident that all men are created equal, that they are endowed by their Creator with certain unalienable Rights, that among these are Life, Liberty, and the pursuit of Happiness. That to

secure these rights, Governments are instituted among Men, deriving
their just powers from the consent of the governed.

This broad and meaningful organ of declaration enabled America to
meet the challenges of a new and mighty nation. This great document
embodies the principle that each human being has value. Its depth of
purport and significance for all people gives the nation sanction to
loosen the shackles of slavery and eventually establish the realization
that all men must be treated as equals and that the fight against injustice
and prejudice must be waged against those who foster these iniquities.

The Declaration of Independence qualifies the people of our nation
to make decisions on government issues. Our founding fathers implied
the belief in the correlation of the growth of democracy and education
for all. Freedom also implies the right of all humans to attain knowledge,
which can be accomplished through education. Through the schools
young people may develop to the extent that they may question the
teachings of the schools and press for those essentials of learning which
will mandate to all who come after them. The premise that our country
requires a concern for the welfare of all of its citizens through the
development of a special consciousness that would make each American
embody a concern for the public welfare was not being implemented in
1964 as stated in an article in *A Handbook on Current Educational Affairs*
entitled "The Shape of Education for 1964" reminds us: "As evidence of
our society's deficiencies in social responsibility, the Commission points
out that many citizens remain indifferent to the well-being of others; that
racial and religious prejudices persist; that millions of disadvantaged
Americans are herded into slums, denied the good schools they need and
the mood models they should have for emulation."

As we discuss desegregation, we, of necessity, discuss integration, for
they both have a bearing on each other. What is desegregation? What is a
racially desegregated school?

Dr. James Boyer, associate professor, Curriculum and Instruction,
College of Education, Kansas State University, defines a segregated
society as "one which denounces the physical separation of human
beings solely on the basis of race, ethnic identity, sex, economic standing, religious preference and the like. The desegregated society is that
dimension which must precede an integrated society."

Many other definitions have been proposed. One is that any school
that is open to all children regardless of race is desegregated. Based on
the proportion of majority or minority group, children enrolled in a
school are in a desegregated setting. Some may call a school with one
black child desegregated; most definitions, however, are more realistic in
which a specification of a certain percentage is given, for example, not

more than 90 percent of the pupils be of one race or that not more than 50 percent be minority group members.

Another definition rejects fixed quotas and suggests the ethnic components of the nation, state or community should be reflected in the ethnic composition of the school. Thus, a desegregated school is a "racially balanced" school, one in which there is proportionate representation of each racial group.

Rather than the consideration of exact definitions, it is relevant and more important in a consideration of outcomes for student development, sound interpersonal relationships and a healthy understanding of people of all backgrounds and understanding to treat each other with equality and respect; to associate and interact as equals with equal rights and opportunities.

Integration means living together, working together, free association with others whose racial composition is different. The desegregation movement itself is not a creator of violence or a particular of unmitigated fear and traumatic upsurges of revolt. The violence, problems, feelings and attitudes of ambivalence generated in schools have not been due to the integration itself but the resistance to integration. As integration progressed in a junior high school in a western city as late as the early 1970s, some black parents and white parents had advised their children not to take any abuse from their classmates of the opposite race and the blacks were prone to harbor this attitude toward teachers also. Resulting occurrences were racial disruptions in the manner of fights, pushing and shoving in the corridors and name-calling. Some blacks and whites seemed to have a chip on their shoulders just waiting for someone to unsettle its equilibrium. However, with special meetings for parents and students by the board of education and the orientation programs at the school and with appropriate counseling, understanding and adjustment education, a settling prevailed and the process of working, learning and association experienced in the process of educational integration proceeded smoothly and with very few interruptions and outbreaks that could be attributed to racial causes. Today, the interaction among the many racial groups in the school is smooth and without problems of consequence.

Many problematic situations arising from integration have manifested innumerable stresses upon teachers and school personnel in the attempt to balance the ratios of teachers within schools, transfer of teachers who did not desire changes to other schools, changes in curriculum to accommodate student needs and dealing with problems involving busing. Many of these changes have been difficult to accept particularly by traditionists and racially prejudiced die-hards who have been inculcated in the cultural continuity of their forefathers. Some of these changes have also affected some blacks who have felt at some time that their fore-fathers were treated unjustly by whites of earlier generations, thus they had to pay for this treatment.

Nearly two decades after the Civil Rights Act outlawing segregation in housing, many black families continue to be threatened, intimidated, looted and burned when moving into white neighborhoods; and although the process of integration is progressing more smoothly black students are often discriminated against, demeaned and harassed on entering predominantly white schools. Adding to the teachers' frustrations and ambivalent problems of a technologically caustic age are the problems of school busing. Although there are different opinions on busing, in April, 1971, the United States Supreme Court held that busing as a means of achieving racial integration in public schools is proper; thus was upheld the decision by federal judges who had ordered busing to implement the intent of the 1954 Supreme Court decision which held that it was inherently unequal to maintain separate educational facilities for Negroes and whites. Also, the Supreme Court permitted a decision by a federal judge in Chicago to be upheld in ordering the Chicago Housing Authority to build public housing in predominantly white neighborhoods with three black families being placed in such neighborhoods for every one white family. While all such legislation and changes have had effects upon teachers, they also have had effects upon children, some good and some even termed "dire."

Many students, even very young ones, must leave home, often in the dark, stand on street corners and at times tolerate the rigors of the elements—snow and rain—even hazard the possibilities of molestation, mugging and kidnapping, as they wait for buses to transport them some-times ten or more miles to an integrated school. This, however, is not a new situation, particularly for blacks in some areas of the United States. In Kansas City, Kansas, before the Supreme Court decision outlawing desegregation in 1954, blacks bypassed "all-white" secondary schools as they used public transit systems to reach an "all-black" junior high school and an "all-black" senior high school ten or more miles from their own homes. Many elementary students alike passed "all-white" schools to get to the ones they attended. Mostly the "all-black" elementary schools proximated the black child's own neighborhood. Although problems have arisen with desegregation and integration, teachers, parents and students have felt its effects in one way or another; it has given rise to the founding fathers intentions that "all men are created equal"; therefore, as time moves on problems become minimal and society is accepting the fact that all humans have rights and privileges.

In reviewing the effects of desegregated schools on pupil achievement, the study *Equality of Educational Organization* revealed that in desegregated schools black pupils benefited greatly while the level of achievement of whites did not decline. It also was found that white children who began attending integrated schools at an early age valued their association with black students, and that the white students who would choose all-white classes or all-white friends were those who first attended classes with nonwhites in the earliest grades and were among the smallest percentage of white students in the survey.

3

Education: Its Meaning and Development

Education is the development of an individual for living and for the successful adjustment to one's environment. Through education, in which learning is intended to be evoked, an individual develops abilities and patterns of thought which determine his attitudes and behavior. Education includes the experiences an individual has, chosen or unsolicited, in his lifetime which determine his actions for good, for bad or for a combination of good and bad. A person is educated not only by his incidental or chosen experiences, but he also is subjected to a social process controlled by his family, his school, his environment and the community life about him. It is through educational experiences that individuals achieve the ability to live and maneuver during their lifetime. The school is the agency through which skills, knowledge and emotional stability are developed, maintained and enlarged. As a result of education, one is expected to conduct himself for good in the social confines of our societal environment according to acceptable standards and mores of that society.

Education, in whatever manner that befits a culture, may be viewed as the means of the transmission of the mores and accumulative knowledge of that culture. Through education a child learns about his culture, molds his attitudes and behavior to conform to the society in which he interacts.

According to Webster education is "the discipline of mind and character through study or instruction; also, a stage of such a process or the training in it. A science dealing with the principles and practices of teaching and learning."

Out of early Roman and Greek civilizations come some of the educational and philosophical thinking of all times. Plato, a Greek philosopher of the third and fourth centuries before the birth of Christ and a teacher of Aristotle and a student of Socrates, stressed unity and harmony above all else and based this assumption upon the existence of a universal principle for all forms. He believed that the chief good synonymous with truth is the highest principle. He contended that only through knowledge could the contemplation of good be possible; therefore, he felt that knowledge educes from opinion to reason which instigates laws, to intuition which sees the universe in its totalness. He believed virtue to be the basis of all human action and that knowledge or learning is the discernment of the general pattern which a particular thing embodies. Plato maintained further that "a good education consists in giving to the body and to the soul all the beauty and all the perfection of which they are capable."

Socrates (469–399 B.C.), said to be the greatest Greek philosopher, was born in Athens and lived during the time of his great teacher, Plato. He had as his educational theme "know thyself." He believed in the oneness of virtue and knowledge. It is virtue, he said, that leads to right habits while knowledge or education, as we know it, gives us a correct picture of man, the universe and God.

Horace Mann, an American educator and champion of educational reform, affirmed that "education alone can conduct us to that enjoyment which is, at once, best in quality and infinite in quantity."

Other principles of education follow:

"Education aims at the realization of the typical man."
        —Payne
"The end of education is triple: to develop mental faculties, to communicate knowledge, to mold characters."
        —Thiry
"Education is the development of the whole man."
        —Comenius
"I call a complete and generous education that which fits a man to perform justly, skillfully, and magnanimously all the offices, both private and public, of peace and war."
        —Milton
"Education is a process of living and not a preparation for future living."
        —John Dewey
"Education is concerned with the development of human beings."
        —Gordon M. Seely

The Means of Transmitting Education

The family unit is the dominant factor in the child's development. It is here that he gains his initial experiences and recognizes the attitudes, values and customs of his social environment. The child's parental involvement and his parents' attitudes on race, religion and social influences of their community are the means by which these attitudes, values and customs are transmitted to him. The parents set the standard for social interactions and human relationships.

Religion and religious elements influence educational practices. Denominational schools such as those sponsored predominantly by the Roman Catholic Church and colleges sponsored for the most part by religious groups play an important part in the progress and perpetuation of education. Examples of colleges that are church sponsored are Rockhurst College, Kansas City, Missouri, and St. Mary's College, Leavenworth, Kansas, both sponsored by the Roman Catholic Church; Baker University, Baldwin, Kansas, by the Methodist Church; Ottawa University, Ottawa, Kansas, and William Jewell College, Liberty, Missouri, by the Baptists; Oakwood College, Huntsville, Alabama, by the Seventh-Day Adventists; and Lane College, Jackson, Tennessee, by the Christian Methodist Episcopal Church (CME).

Communication media, encompassing radio, television and newspapers, exercise a tremendous influence on the educational thought of a nation and its people. Informational programs—including national and international world affairs, aesthetic presentations, political debates, contests and classical operas and dramatic programs—have influenced our educational thinking and growth. Newspapers, magazines, books and the access to excellent library facilities have all added to our vocational, literary and leisure-time training and activities. While these substances are educational, for the most part, they add many hours of entertainment and diversity to our usual routines. Through reading one gains vicarious experiences even though the actual experiences are beyond our capabilities to attain or even void of our desire to experience. Various vocations and occupations in which we are engaged afford us opportunities for learning and for extending and expanding our associations.

The economy exerts an immeasurable impact on education. The type of educational system that a city, county or state has, the school buildings, teacher pay and the private and state support are dependent, to a great extent, on the existing economic level and financial base of the community.

Motion pictures and travel also increase educational growth. Through these media we accumulate knowledge of people, places and events that would otherwise be unavailable to us. Various industries in a locality which provide a livelihood for its constituency are sources of educational knowledge. Through an understanding of the industry, how it affects the people engaged in it and the impact it exerts on the economic growth of the community all have educational value.

Many other educational factors for growth and learning, such as technological advances in space, in machinery, in medical and physical progress, add to the cultural level and advancement of educational thought and reach far beyond the classroom.

Poverty, wars, protests, strikes, racial conflicts and changes, political activities, heavy crimes and violence have a pronounced effect on the thinking and growth of a people. Education, therefore, is not confined to the confines of a classroom; rather, we may say education is multifaceted and pluralistic.

A History of Education

The history of education throughout the ages has been a series of complex developments. Its growth has not been steady and consistent from early times. The individual at times was subordinated to the church or the state. Similarly, in some countries, education was mostly conducted as such in the religious affairs while in other countries education was secular or nonecclesiastical and not under the control of the church. Through the centuries education changed from student activity to the lecture method, from craft apprenticeship to the memorization of Latin phrases by children. The instruction vacillated from one type to another. Since the present educational systems of learning contain vestiges of ancient, medieval and early modern European systems of learning, in order to trace the history of education, one must review these systems. A child wherever born is void of culture. It is the process of education which shapes his attitudes and behavior and fits him to grow and live in society. This learning process may be rooted in the home, in the school or transmitted through centuries by word of mouth.

In many primitive societies education is merely a process of cultural transmission or enculturation, as it is called. Their culture is transmitted from one generation to another with little change as the life models are static and absolute. In many of these primitive societies, children participate in the processes of adult activities and, as Margaret Mead, an American anthropologist, says in *Coming of Age in Samoa,* learning is based upon empathy, identification and imitation. By observing and emulating basic practices, primitive children learn before reaching puberty. Their immediate community and their family are their teachers. Since many persons within a household have a part in rearing these Samoan offspring, it is noted that the dependence on parents which is attendant to close affectional ties is not as great as in the American culture. Margaret Mead in her book states:

The close relationship between parent and child, which has such a decisive influence upon so many in our civilization, that submission to the parent may become the dominating pattern of a lifetime, is not found in Samoa. Children reared in households where there are a half dozen adult women to care for them and dry their tears, and a half dozen adult males, all of whom represent constituted authority, do not distinguish their parents as sharply as our children do. The image of the fostering, loving mother, or the admirable father, which may serve to determine affectional choices later in life, is a composite affair; composed of several aunts, cousins, older sisters and grandmothers; of chief, father, uncles, brothers and cousins. Instead of learning as its first lesson that here is a kind mother whose special and principal care is for its welfare, and a father whose authority is to be deferred to, the Samoan baby learns that its world is composed of a hierarchy of male and female adults, all of whom can be depended upon and must be deferred to.

Margaret Mead elaborates further on the effect of the many family members who have a part in a Samoan child's development:

They are schooled not by an individual but by an army of relatives into a general conformity upon which the personality of their parents has a very slight effect. And through an endless chain of cause and effect, individual differences of standard are not perpetuated through the children's adherence to the parents' position, nor are children thrown into bizarre, untypical attitudes which might form the basis for departure and change.

Since early times as cultures have become more complex and the accumulation of knowledge reaches beyond the comprehension of any individual, a new means of transmitting culture must be made; thus has come about formal education, the school and the educational authority, the teacher. Hence, with the growth of education have come many philosophies, objectives and methods for making teaching more effective and education more meaningful. The formal atmosphere of the school with set areas of instruction and definite curriculum to insure learning is more definitive than by imitation and observation.

Early Civilizations and Cultural Development

In the Near East, particularly in Egypt and Mesopotamia, the history of the earliest civilizations began about 3000 B.C. About a millennium and a half, which is 1,500 years later, the North China civilization began. While the highly developed civilization of Egypt and Mesopotamia contained differences, both evoked literary achievements of great diversity and merit. To perpetuate these civilizations there arose a need for formal education.

Civilizations of the Old World

Egypt and Mesopotamia

The priests who were the intelligentsia of the Egyptian government were the controllers of culture and education. They were the teachers in the formal schools of the humanities which included those subjects which dealt with the characteristics of human life: classical courses in literature, philosophy, languages and religion. These priests also taught useful subjects of science, mathematics, medicine and geometry. Two types of schools were developed under the supervision of officials of government and priests and were restricted to the youth of the elite; one of the schools was for priesthood training and the other for scribes. Religion and education were practiced together. Strict discipline, memorization, drill and sternness were employed. Harsh punishment was meted out to the indolent. Just as the education of the Egyptians, Mesopotamian formal education was directed toward the training of scribes and priests. This training was in the basics of religion, reading and writing to subjects in astrology, medicine and law. Scribes became librarians, copyists and teachers. The intellectual and educational training was left primarily to the priests. The hub of intellectual learning was the library, which was located in a temple. Stressed were oral repetition, memorization and copying of models and scripts.

Old World Civilization in North China

Unlike the education in the early civilizations of Egypt and Mesopotamia, education in North China, which began with the Shang era, was nonreligious or secular and highly moralistic in nature. Their education stressed moral responsiveness and duty toward people and the state. Rituals, music and cooperative relations with one another formed the basis of their education. They received their moral training through word of mouth in the many rituals they performed and through the use of bamboo books. Early education was not compulsory and only the instruction in the colleges of the large cities was provided by the state. These provisions were primarily in the forms of competitive examinations for admission to public office.

The New World Civilization

Mayans, Aztecs and Incas

These "aborigines" of the New World were so called by some because of the misconception of Columbus, who felt his newly-discovered land was India and its inhabitants the Indians of the Eastern Hemisphere. A high degree of civilization had been attained by these tribes living in Peru, Colombia, Central America, Yucatan and Mexico. Among the Mexican tribes were the celebrated Aztecs, a powerful and cultured people. It is documented that they formed a closely knit empire which dominated most of Mexico and included Guatemala, El Salvador and Nicaragua. The Mayans lived in Yucatan and Central America. Hailing from the highlands of South America, mostly in Peru, were the Incas. The pre-Colombian civilizations of the Mayans, Aztecs and Incas, while not too distinctively documented, revealed that these people developed a type of training for the priesthood and for those of noble birth. Noteworthy of these Mayan people was the development of a calendar which indicated their broad knowledge of mathematics and astronomy. Highly important, too, was the calendar of the Incas and their construction of superb roads and buildings made of massive stone blocks. In the Inca civilization the government took over every child and supervised vocational training and socialization.

Education for these Indians was in rituals and curricula directed toward the three classes of nobility. These classes included the tribal chiefs or the curacas, the imperial ayllus and the upper-class common Indians. The cuzco was the learning center where the sons of the ayllus and the curacas were educated for a period of four years. The language of the nobility was learned the first year; this was the Quechua language. Religion was studied the second year, and the third year was devoted to the "quipus," which was a complicated method of sending messages and making records of historical events. Rigorous examinations concluded this education for full Inca nobility stature.

The magnificence of the temples of the Aztecs and the renowned writing systems of the Maya are demonstrations of their vast accomplishments. The Mayans placed character training as the most powerful element in their education. Cultural conservation, vocational training and moral and character training constituted the purposes of their education.

Classical Cultures and Their Educational Development

India

One of the most ancient civilizations in the world is attributed to India. Religion was the all-encompassing feature of education, government, law, philosophy and morality in addition to the all-engulfing prayer and worship with which these people were synonymous. The education in this civilization consisted of various stages engaged in by children at different age levels. Instruction was given in the home up to the age of seven, at the school from eight to sixteen and finally at the university. The initial and primary learning period began at home, and formal or secondary education began with a ritual called the "up-anayana" or thread ceremony. Ages for the secondary learning stage differed according to castes and were compulsory for the three higher castes. In the three castes, the Brahmin started this ceremony at eight years of age, the Ksatriya at the age of eleven and the Vaisya children began at the age of twelve years. The male child left home for this secondary stage of education and moved to the home of his preceptor or teacher. The preceptor's home was the "asrama," which was located in the forest or woods, and the teacher was known as the "acarya." The acarya treated the student as his own son, charged him no room and board and gave him a free education. The student, of course, was given chores about the house and tended the sacrificial fires of the rituals. Schooling including the study of grammar and science, and a definite group of studies was mandatory for a young man of the priestly class. He was obliged to possess a knowledge of the Vedas, which were three of the ancient Hindu scriptures, and he also was obligated to follow the dress of brahmacarya, which was the ultimate in simplicity; he lived on the most common fare and led a life of celibacy, remaining unmarried during this period.

Education of this type usually lasted for twelve years, but students who desired to continue their education could leave the forest school (asrama), enter a university and pursue higher studies in philosophy at an academy or a "parisad."

Toward the end of the sixth century B.C., the method of education changed. The Brahmanic system emerged, bringing into being the two new religious orders of Buddhism and Jainism. Vedic literature from early times had been vital to these Hindus; however, these two groups repudiated the authority and their right of the Brahmins to priesthood. The founders of these religions did not discriminate according to caste, sex or creed and gave education to all in a common manner understood by all. The Buddhists brought about the monastic system of education which could not include everyone, only the ones to be educated for the priesthood; these aspirants to the priesthood lived in monasteries. Following the death of Asoka, India's revered ruler, a lay movement as a result of Hindu resistance and a counterreformation in Hinduism was brought about. A great impact was made on elementary, secondary and higher learning. The inclusion of secular or nonecclesiastical education as well as the retention of religious education were resultants of these events.

By the close of the eighth century outstanding strides were made by the Indian civilization as was evident in the appearance of Nalanda and Valabhi universities and the resurgence of interest in the sciences, mathematics and medicine.

Because of trade relations and through the interchange of Indian and Chinese scholars in Asia, the Indian culture had a great deal of influence on Asia. Ancient China's education specified the molding of character as its principal aim with emphasis on moral and ethical standards.

The Hebrew Influence upon Educational Advancement

Jewish education stressed exactness and preciseness. Like many other cultures, education in ancient Israel was carried on through the teaching of the mother to the girls and the father's teaching to the boys. Education included the training of scribes in the art of writing. Because of the scribe's ability to write, he was entrusted with many administrative duties, and he also was given character training and guidance in developing wisdom. Oral education still held sway, however, over writings. Sacred laws were written and learned by heart. Eventually these oral and written laws were written in books which ultimately called for an extended program of instruction. These programs included elementary, intermediate and advanced stages. This educational advancement was important in the survival of Judaism. With the destruction of Jerusalem, the Jewish people retained their language of worship, Hebrew.

Greek Civilization

The European origins of education remain historically significant today. Although the present American schools are unlike any European educational system, such influences may be seen in the Greek educational system where in Sparta and Athens, before formal education came into being, education was carried on within the family group. Early education in most civilizations was dominated by religious influences; however, secular education was the practice in other civilizations with emphasis on the person rather than on the church or state.

Greek civilization will be considered here as pre-Hellenic, Hellenic and Hellenistic. The Mycenaean civilization of about 1400–1100 B.C. supposedly begins the history and development of the Hellenic people. Mycenae, a town in ancient Greece situated at the northern portion of the plain of Argos, is, especially in the stories of Homer, as the city of

Agamemnon. This ancient civilization was preceded by the pre-Hellenic civilization of Minoan Crete. It is said to have been governed by nobility; thus, as were other cultures so directed, their education was assumed to be for the scribes, who were the writers and copiers of manuscripts. Conflicts and upheavals existed throughout Athenian history between the upper and lower classes. Political disorder or anarchy and the rule of a tyrannical or oppressive ruler were constantly prevalent. Following the Greek dark ages, which historians dated from the eleventh to the ninth centuries B.C., at which time little was known of the Greek civilization, a new civilization emerged. A military aristocracy headed the society of this time, one as exemplified in Homer's *Iliad* and *Odyssey*. The nobility was educated by the teachings and advice of the older men. Throughout this period of education, a mutual understanding and an ideal of Greek love characterized the Hellenic civilization and its form of education.

The Hellenic Period

Sparta

In Sparta, one of the most colorful and thriving cities of Greece, one sees an elevated level of aesthetic refinement in education in the religious festivals held in the city. Education was an instrument of the state for its own benefit. Training of the males was for the military. Physical training for girls had as its main objective physical strength for bearing strong male children who would eventually become competent soldiers who would be obedient, capable and of long duration. There evolved a cult of military and sporting groups in which individuals could gain self-confidence, competitive skills and acclaim and prestige. The cult of Homer constituted the foundations of Greek culture and education; this dedication to the high competitiveness in performance in the arena characterized the Olympic games, which date from 776 B.C.

The city-state became all-important in the new political transformation; thus emphasis was on the military and the subordination of the city to the state. Both boys and girls took part in physical education as they participated in Olympic games. Military and civic education, therefore, played a significant part in protecting their lands. It was around 550 B.C. when military training was most prolific. Agoge, or education, lasted from the ages of seven to twenty for the boys; this education was completely controlled by the state, and the young men were trained to endure hardships and pain and even to die if need be for the defense of Sparta. Weak, sickly and deformed children were put to death. The education in Sparta, because of its bold militaristic and puritanical adherence to obedience to the state, enabled this civilization to become the most powerful of all Greek nations diplomatically and militarily, but with poverty of intellectual progress. Unlike Athens, Sparta left no legacy of thought.

Athens

Athens, the capital city of Greece, had as its dominating feature the Acropolis; it is hailed as the earliest seat of the Athenian kings. The ancient Greeks worshiped gods, and their beliefs and magnificent temples and shrines made these gods realistic to the Greek people of that time and today include traces of realism to followers and students of Greek mythology. In 480–79 B.C.these ancient temples and shrines were destroyed, but under the rulers Themistocles, Cimon and Pericles, the Acropolis—on a low hill in the center of the plain on which Athens is located and standing some 300 feet above the town—together with the ruins now standing are considered among the most magnificent treasures in the world today. Thousands of travelers visit Greece each year and marvel at their beauty.

Just as in Sparta, education was predominantly in the interest of the state; however, withstanding this fact, the education in Athens extended beyond that of the military. Other instruction was given to boys of seven and older in music, reading and writing. Social behavior was introduced to the boys by an elderly slave or "paedadgogus," who became the boys' companion at all times. At an exercising ground called a "palaestra," physical education was engaged in. Additional training between the ages of fifteen and eighteen was given outside the city at a "gymnasia." Each boy became a soldier at the age of eighteen and at twenty, a citizen. Character development with emphasis on moral and ethical training was as important as the learning of subjects.

Socrates

Interest in sports lessened and with Socrates (470–399 B.C.) and his contemporaries, and the Sophists, his adversaries, a great interest arose in debate, politics, public speaking and systems of higher education to all who could afford it and who had the leisure time to pursue it. With them were started lectures through which young men were helped to learn philosophy and to understand the individual's relation to society. Poetry and prose were the bases of the literary culture. This literary culture held sway through the centuries and eventually became mostly theoretical. Astronomy was the only mathematical study that remained in favor.

The Sophists, Socrates' antagonists and opposers, challenged the absolute standards of morality and the relativity of truth. They stressed the art of public speaking and became the first lawyers of modern civilization. As opposed to the Sophists' thinking, Socrates believed that truth was absolute and that truth did exist. The teacher, according to him, was the leader of civilization. Socrates became the supreme model for later education and was the greatest of the Greek philosophers. He believed everyone needed education—the rich and the poor, the intelligent and the slow, the old as well as the young.

Plato

Plato (427–347 B.C.) was a Greek philosopher and a teacher of Aristotle. He did not undertake to educate men. He accepted no fees and his conversations were open to all. His *Dialectic* was presented as a series of dramas through which the dialogues proceed with questions and answers. Plato believed there existed a universal principal for all forms. Ideas to him were what were real, not individuals; these ideas were believed to be external, unchanging and perfect.

Plato became a disciple of Socrates at the age of twenty, which was approximately eight or nine years before Socrates' death. Plato possessed an uncanny ability to ask questions which searched men's souls as he proclaimed the only knowledge which he had was an awareness of his own ignorance. Although he offered no doctrine, his acute, precise and humbling questioning created much disfavor among the pedagogues or teachers in Athens. To him, there existed a universal principle for all forms, and he contended that unity and harmony were important above all else; that good was identical with truth; that good was possible only through knowledge; that virtue led to correct habits; and that knowledge gave a correct picture of man, the universe and God. He felt that virtue, which is dependent upon knowledge, was the basis of all human action; and knowledge, considered by him to be the most important virtue, was the discernment of the pattern which a certain thing embodied or its perception in relation to its universal idea. This is the embodiment of his "Doctrine of Ideas," wherein all definite ideas or finite experiences share eternal qualities which become universals.

Plato wielded a great impact upon education, and all of his beliefs appear to be inspired by the educational standards of Sparta. To him, the state represented the highest concerns of the individual. He stressed the importance of learning in his educational levels. He projected the idea of the importance of education in infancy to the age of three when youngsters could develop good habits through example. He also stressed imparting the idea of bravery at this age as being very important. From three to six, disciplinary measures would be used freely if needed. Boys were separated from girls at ages six to thirteen and hence afterward their association would be with boys only. He saw the need for the inclusion of more exacting education in instrumental music, poetry and mathematics; and from the ages of sixteen to twenty boys should be exposed to military training and strenuous physical exercise.

This great philosopher believed in the importance of individual differences, that the same training could not be used for all, that the superior students should not be neglected in education and that women should essentially receive the same education as men. In addition to intelligence, he cited peace, prosperity and happiness as being achieved by the rule of the "wisest," and good government as being dependent upon the more important factors of morality and dedication to the welfare of others.

Historians point out two weaknesses of this great Greek philosopher: Plato envisioned an educational Utopia, and he had contempt for the masses.

Philosophical Thinking: Its Meaning, Characteristics and Systems

In studying and discussing education and the philosophies of men of early and classical civilizations which influenced its principles and development, it is well to pause briefly to analyze the thought processes, characteristics and methods of these philosophers, for through them have come some of the most far-reaching and profound postulations that have given rise to change, encouraged thinking and produced inestimable progress in education, in its methods and in its assimilation.

The Greek words "philos," which means "lover," and "sophia," which means "wisdom," compose the word "philosophy." Thus, we may say that a philosopher is a lover of wisdom. Wisdom is the result of long reflection and disciplined thinking; it is the ability to analyze, to assimilate, to make inferences; and it is the discernment of undercurrents which are not always easily seen or understood, but which make things what they are. The philosopher's range of thought is boundless and diversified; he looks at the entire world, a life, and seeks its purpose,meanings and even goes beyond the physical realm. He has a curiosity about the earth, how it began, how it will end; he also wonders about man, about the hereafter. Is there a God? He asks: Why, How, What? The philosopher is a questioner, a thinker, an interpreter, an analyzer, a reflective and disciplined mind. He could be called a mastermind, a studier of the abstract, one who thinks beyond the normal patterns of the mind's comprehension. To simplify the philosopher's vast store of knowledge and not to become confused with the preponderance of his acquired knowledge, the philosopher assimilates his materials, giving particular names to particular questions and specific terminology

to specific views. When a question is related to the origin and development of the world, the subject is known as cosmogony. When a question
concerns the nature of a thing or the source from which everything
comes, it is called ontology. Advocates of ontology differ in their beliefs
and views. Those who believe the world is one are monists. Some believe
in two realities and are known as dualists. Idealists believe reality is
essentially spiritual or the embodiment of mind or reason, and they
believe the world is fundamental beyond the spirit, and that the universe
is explained by the existence of matter. The dynamists subscribe to the
belief that energy or force is the ultimate physical reality, and those who
believe in a neutrality of the world, beyond mind, matter and energy, are
known as neutralists.

Should matters of inquiry concern human knowledge possibilities, it
is known as epistemology. If the subject concerns ideals of human living,
good or bad conduct, right or wrong, it is called ethics. Concerning
beauty, the study is aesthetics, and logic deals with the processes of the
mind's reasoning powers, the ability to draw conclusions, to make decisions and to analyze ideas relative to each other.

Many terms used by philosophers had their beginnings with early
classical Greek thinkers who were progenitors or forerunners of Western
civilization. Metaphysics, which refers to all questions collectively dealing with matters beyond the physical world or physical nature, is one
such word used by the Greeks.

Aristotle

Aristotle (384–322 B.C.) was a disciple of Socrates and an outstanding
Greek philosopher and tutor of Alexander the Great. While Plato was
concerned with the improvement of life, Aristotle was concerned with
understanding life and things. Called a Stagirite because he was born at
Stagira, a Greek colonial town on the coast of Macedonia, Aristotle
wrote and lectured on science and philosophy including biology, physics,
astronomy, logic, psychology, metaphysics, ethics and politics. The foundations of all the sciences and branches of philosophy today are attributed to Aristotle. Plato accepted reincarnation and believed that life
after death was determined by life on earth, while Aristotle did not
adhere to a belief in personal survival after death. To him, man's intellect was made up of active and passive reason and that the passive reason
became extinct with death but the active reason was immortal. He
favored the cultivation of the intellect and believed that only through the
use of time could these intellectual powers be developed. He felt that the
state was the fulfillment of man's drives; therefore, the state was in

charge of education, and education should have as a main objective the training of citizens. Classification and structure were all-important.

Aristotle asserted that the systematization of young people's education should involve physical development in the following stages: from birth to seven, learning to endure hardships; from seven to puberty to include fundamentals of music, reading, writing, gymnasium and enumeration; and in the next stage, which included puberty to age seventeen, the youth would be concerned with learning the exact knowledge of science, literature, mathematics and music. Only the superior students were to engage in higher education with interests in biological and physical sciences. The Lyceum, Aristotle's school, was more empirical than Plato's Academy. Aristotle is considered a bridge from the Hellenic age of Greek civilization to the Hellenistic age. This great philosopher sanctioned the belief that the ultimate reality of anything is an idea and that the world consists of substances, each existing in itself. He distinguished between matter and form, between the actual and the potential, and believed that in this world exists a purpose and God is its first cause and final objective. Aristotle's greatness lies in his emphasis upon reason. He was a symbol of Athenian life with a balanced concept of man and his intellectual powers with stress on moderation. Education, according to him, was concerned with the development of all aspects of man's capabilities, moral, intellectual and physical.

The death of Aristotle brought an end to the Hellenic period. The period that followed, the Hellenistic age, evidenced a drastic change in the general thinking and a decline in philosophy.

The Hellenistic Age

In the Hellenistic period, rather than emphasizing objective views of reality and of the social and communal ideal of the city-state, the person or individual became the main concern. Although Hellenism was eventually eroded by the Persian national renaissance in the Near East and the invasions from Central Asia in the second century B.C., its basic foundation of the individual, the conflict between skepticism and religion, between faith and reason, continued to increase and expand under Roman domination into the Mediterranean world. Its educational pattern persisted and was likened to the Greeks in that it was directed mostly to the male nobility. It was dependent upon the city; gymnastics formed the foundation of training. Emphasis on educational sports declined in favor of literary studies.

In the primary schools, harsh discipline was the rule in the school of letters where Latin and poor methods of teaching slowed and made

difficult the learning process. The educative process in primary, secondary and higher learning was slow and lacked institutionalization and
creativity. Although this Hellenistic age depended upon other cultures
for ideas and theories, they, nevertheless, were ingenuous in technological advancements; and scholars of merit added much to this culture.
Archimedes contributed to physics and mathematics; in technology Hero
of Alexandria was notable; and other great men included Euclid and
Appollonius in mathematics; Ptolemy, Aristarchus and Hipparchus in
astronomy; and in geography worthy of note was Eratosthenes, Strabo
and Posidonius. In technology, Hero of Alexandria was important. Historically, Greek progress could have been made in this age had scholars
used their own ideas, imagination and viewpoints rather than dwelling
on a limited social class system which negated intellectual articulation of
thought and encouraged luxurious living and dwelled heavily on the
splendor of the past.

Rome

The home was the principal source of early education in Rome. The
mother's influence predominated and often extended beyond the early
years. At the age of seven boys' education and development were exclusively under the father's guidance in a strict and exacting manner.
Education in the family with the father ended at the age of sixteen for the
male. He was apprenticed to a family friend and finally entered military
service.

Education in Rome paralleled that in Greece; thus the Romans
adopted the Hellenistic education, and the programs, methods and institutions were transposed into Latin. Art, music and gymnastics for
health and the Roman course of study all embodied Greek similarities.
Three types of education developed. On the elementary level reading
and writing were taught by the "litterator." Between the third and the
end of the first centuries B.C. the secondary level, the "grammaticus
Latinus"— corresponding to the Greek "grammatikos"—was developed.
In higher education, schools of rhetoric were developed. The explication
of poetry was the main object of this education, which was slow to rise
because of the delayed development of Latin literature. The Greek
influence became significant as Rome developed. Livius Andronicus, a
Greek scholar after 272 B.C., came to Rome and transposed the *Odyssey*
into Latin; Plautus translated Greek comedy themes and Cato, the
Censor, attempted to curb the influence of Greek literature and thought.

To counter the aristocratic education of the Greeks, the Romans
practiced the art of combining philosophical thought, viewpoints and
doctrines, which became known as eclecticism. With the appearance of

the work of Cicero (104–43 B.C.), who was concerned with rhetoric, the science of public speaking gained prominence. The discourses of Cicero were the counterparts of those of Demosthenes, the Greek orator, and Cicero's treatises eliminated the use of Greek manuals by providing a technical vocabulary.

The Hellenistic origins persisted in the works of the teacher and Roman rhetorician Quintilian (circa A.D. 35–95), but less impregnated with Latin than Cicero's proposals. He believed the teaching of rhetoric to be closely aligned with the art of the lectures. In Quintilian's treatise on rhetoric in twelve books entitled *De Institutione oratorio libra xii or Institutiones oratoriae,* he discussed early education, arrangement, composition and circumstances for oratorical success. Oratory was the most important subject of higher education during this time. Quintilian believed simplicity should be stressed in all stages of educational development, objected to corporal punishment in schools and believed in a type of behavior modification or positive awards.

4

Influences on Ancient Education

Stoicism

An Athenian school of philosophy Stoicism was founded by Zeno of Citium in Cyprus. It appeared after the death of Aristotle. Several exponents of Stoicism expounded its beliefs so earnestly that they also are thought of as its leaders. They were Chrysippus and Panactius of Rhodes. This school of thought was most compatible or in accord with Roman thinking. The men famous for its impact and who may be called exponents of Stoicism included Romans such as Seneca (A.D. 3–65), the Emperor Marcus Aurelius and Epictetus. Although a practical philosophy, it possessed metaphysical as well as ethical views. These exponents believed all reality to be material. In the metaphysical view, two important ethical effects are involved; one, "living according to nature" or "reason," means living in accord with the divine order of the universe; and two, the doctrine that teaches that everything that happens is according to the divine order and is for the best and involves a wide optimism. The Stoics taught that evil had no metaphysical or abstract reality. They believed that mind controlled all emotions and that the true good of man lies not in outward objects, but in the state of the soul itself. A forcefully practical and religious tendency characterized Stoicism of the later or Roman period such as found in the *Discourses of Encheridion* of Epictetus and the *Thoughts or Meditations* of Marcus Aurelius. The Stoics accepted the concept of natural law which was extended to all mankind as they preached the brotherhood of man. Zeno, who was the founder of this theory, thought the souls of the virtuous did not perish after death. Although they did not have a definite theory on immortality, one of its most ardent advocates, Chrysippus, believed the only people to be immortal were the Stoics.

60

Epicureanism

Epicureanism, the philosophy of Epicurus (341–270 B.C.), was another movement which had an influence on education. Devotion to pleasure, comfort and high living forms its basis. Characterizing the philosophy of Epicureanism are some fundamental concepts. One is atomism, held by Democritus, which deals with a spontaneous movement of atoms that affects all forces of the universe and the existence of gods, extraneous or nonessential, to world happenings. This theory maintained that the soul was a body composed of several species of atoms.

Epicurus contended that to have a happy life, one must be "free from pain in the body and from trouble in the mind." To achieve this happiness he believed man must provide himself with security, which could be accomplished in two ways: by reducing his needs to a minimum and withdrawing from the world and human competition, and second, by adding friendship to public laws. These Epicureans appealed not to religion, but to scientific explorations of thought.

Other theories contributed much to education and to the thinking during this period.

Other Philosophical Theories Affecting Educational Thought and Actions

Plutarch (A.D. 46–120), a Greek biographer, is to be remembered for his contributions. His *Parallel Lives* concerns the lives of forty-six famous Greeks and Romans arranged in pairs for comparison of a Greek with a Roman. He contributed to educational theory by his *Moralia, or the Education of Children.* He advocated strict discipline, correct habits and the cultivation of memory.

Neoplatonism

Another philosophy which flourished during the third century and onward in Alexandria and Athens was Neoplatonism. In general, Neoplatonism applies to any group or body which is in accord or aligned with the doctrine founded upon Plato's ethical and metaphysical principles. This Alexandrian school of philosophy and religion, which applied to the elite, was founded by Ammonius Saccas. The consummation or completion and collapse of ancient philosophy may be attributed to the Neoplatonic schools of Alexandria and Athens. Plotinus, pupil of the founder, was its ardent proponent; in his *Enneads* he expounded his most penetrating expressions to the Neoplatonic teachings. In this teaching there existed a supreme principle beyond all reality, the suprarational principle, the One, containing all perfections. From the One arises the Mind, which contemplates the perfections and beauty of the One, and from this evolves the Soul. All forms, both animate and inanimate, that go to make up the universe emanate from this universal soul. According to the most divine Plotinus, real education is dependent upon good citizenship and ethical conduct. Neoplatonism indicates that man's life on earth is essentially transitory and the supreme spirit is supreme.

Many philosophies concerning the world, life and religion abounded during these early times. They made a profound impact on the educational and social thinking of the time and had a bearing on institutions to come. "The philosopher," said Plato, "is the spectator of all time and of all existence."

The doctrines of Neoplatonism were widespread and served as the initial foundation for the development of scholastic philosophy and theology.

Jesus, a Teacher of the Rich and the Poor

Jesus' profound influence on Western educational history is of inestimable significance. His appeal was widespread; he related to the Jesuits, the Quakers, Orthodox believers as well as liberals. He was the founder of the Christian religion; his name means "the anointed one" and the "Messiah." Born of humble circumstances in Bethlehem of Judea, at the age of twelve he was in the temple telling learned men wondrous things; he felt he was called to a heavenly mission and journeyed about preaching "the kingdom of God." Jesus lived to the age of thirty. Those about him were the twelve who were to become his Apostles and a group of seventy who simply went about spreading his teachings.

Although Jesus was sorely misunderstood, the Jews were searching for a redeemer to save them from their oppression by the Romans. The Hebrew religion was legalistic and the Pharisees lacked humility. Jesus was the greatest of all teachers, for he believed and preached the love of all mankind and the importance of the spirit and not earthly possessions; he possessed compassion for all, humility, patience, love for the rich and the poor and for the learned and unlearned, love for all mankind. He preached religion and education to be synonymous. Jesus taught how to find the path to God and how to avoid evil. Like Jesus, teachers must realize the importance of teaching everyone, the rich, the poor, high, low, intelligent and ignorant, black and white and all nationalities as they stress the important factors in life, to gain inner peace, strength and knowledge in grace and understanding to higher ideals of living and to the development of each individual to his highest potential.

Roman Education

Concurrent with the Romanization of the provinces, the Roman empire became a network of schools. The primary schools remained private. Many schools of grammar or rhetoric took on the appearance of public institutions financed by a municipal budget or by private foundations. Roman education retained much of its sameness throughout many centuries in its educational methods and curricula. This continuity existed for 6,000 years in Greek and six or seven centuries in Roman territory. Only the use of Greek and Latin languages changed. Greek became less and less well known. The rise of Latin classics came about; Virgil and Cicero relieved Homer and Demosthenes. In the fourth and fifth centuries the medical terminology of medical education came into being; medical manuals were translated from Greek into Latin.

The new Christian religion usually had special religious education provided by both the church and the family, and the education received in the schools was classical education and shared with the pagans. As time progressed with the Roman society's conversion, Christians became teachers in all areas of education and incorporated the classical education. Christians believed that through the study of Scriptures they could learn what was needed to be known about the world.

The Middle Ages

Historians place the chronological time for the Middle Ages between 476 and 1453, marking the end of the Western or Roman Empire and the fall of the Eastern or Byzantine (Constantinople) Empire. The title "Middle Ages" was used to denote a lessened level of progress between the high levels of civilization. Historians cite the outstanding achievements of this historical period to be in the areas of the power of the feudal lords or the aristocracy who owned lands and the emergence of feudal society and scholastic society. This period produced and bequeathed to modern Western civilization the institutional framework provided through the church and labor groups and the university to the constitutional state. Many of their philosophical concepts of ethics remain with us today.

Invasions of barbarians into imperial territory and the abolition of compulsory military service are among the causes of the decay and subsequent fall of the Roman Empire. War with the barbaric tribes of the

Turko-Tartar Huns and other Germanic tribes, and the greatness and grandeur of Rome, was ended by 500. The eastern half of the empire, with its seat at Byzantium or Constantinople, flourished with Emperor Constantine, its leader and namesake. By thwarting the invasions of the German barbarians a centralized, strong government was set up. This Eastern Empire persevered and endured for almost 400 years. It lost its glory as a great power but served as an appeaser between the Moslem empire of the East and the revived West.

Eventually the beginnings of modern European states arose and the Papacy reached great heights. A great feudal aristocracy began to emerge in Europe, and the battle between the temporal or secular and ecclesiastical powers ensued.

The Christian Church was organized in the latter days of the Roman Empire under a body of ecclesiastics, a hierarchy of bishops and arch-bishops. In most of Europe the leader of the Christian Church was the bishop at Rome and his church became the Roman Catholic Church. Although the civilization of Rome and Greece ended with the overthrow of the Roman Empire by barbarians, the classical writings and various ceremonial practices remained.

Establishment of Schools for the Clergy

With the advent of the Roman Catholic Church there arose a need to establish schools where monks and priests could be trained. The bishop was the overseer of the training preparatory to priesthood, and since the schools were located at the seat of the diocese or bishopric, they became episcopal or cathedral schools.

These bishops' schools were sometimes looked upon as successors of the Roman Empire's grammar schools and are often thought to be the parents of today's grammar or elementary schools. Specialization in the development of the clergy was the main function of these schools; however, the episcopal schools admitted young lay persons later upon the disappearance of the small Roman schools. Some bishops organized a type of boarding school where the students who were aspiring clergy-men lived in a community, performed monastic duties and learned the doctrines of the clergy. The children who were not of the aristocracy, or who were not to become clergymen or monks, received an irregular Christian education.

The schools for the training of priests and monks were the most influential educational institutions of the Middle Ages. Three main types of cathedral schools were in existence. One was the grammar school, which was taught by a canon or clergyman of the cathedral and known as a scholasticus. The cantor or precentor taught the music school and the choristers' school. The catachumenal school, an earlier church school, was used to teach converts to Christianity in the forms and religions of the church. Their purpose was specifically to teach religion. These monastic and cathedral schools preserved some traces of Greek and Roman civilization. These church schools, by a decree of Justinian in 529, were the only schools permitted to exist and as a result a new philosophic movement developed. It was called "scholasticism" because of its relation to the "doctors scholasticus" of the church schools.

Boys up to ten years of age could be admitted to monastic schools to become monks. Because of the long time commitment to the end, many gave up. Girls attended schools similar to those of the boys; the girls' schools were held in convents. Reading, writing and computation comprised the curriculum of the monastic schools in the early Middle Ages. Several eminent scholars lived during this time. Isidore of Seville (560–636), in his *Etymologies,* attempted to classify knowledge in an encyclopedia; Alcuin, a scholar in charge of a palace school of Charlemagne (742–814), is credited with composing a syllabus or a type of course of study prepared for Charlemagne's son, Pepin.

Charlemagne, historians say, was the creator of medieval education. He demanded the clergy to be educated severely as he promoted ecclesiastical and educational reform. As a result of his influence, the churchmen emerged with high moral standards and higher educational standards than before.

The Renaissance

A Revival of Learning and the Humanists

A revival of learning during the Renaissance was seen principally in England, Italy, France, Germany and Spain. During this period Western man was able to resist and reject the two institutions of the Middle Ages, namely economic and political feudalism and the Church. In the Renaissance period nationalism's rise was experienced and explorations were made. Among the discoveries that were made was the possession of the Canary Islands by the Spaniards in the fourteenth century. New approaches to philosophy developed, and the emergence of new literature, the appearance of new writers, and architecture, painting and sculpture came to the fore. Art became the major medium of interpretation. Women played an important role in the development of culture and in the advancement of learning. Man, too, was glorified and the conception of a gentleman was cultivated; he loved education and held a desire to cultivate the sciences and art.

Humanism

A new interest, Humanism, in which there was a revived interest in studies dealing with man, his abilities and desires, appeared near the end of the Middle Ages. It implied an abiding interest in humanity. The word "humanism" comes from the Latin "studia humanitatis." At the time of this movement's beginning the focus solely in religion was ended. Humanistic study was envisioned in the fourteenth century as seen in the works of Petrarch and Boccaccio. Knowledge, according to the Humanists, had as its major emphasis the solving of problems pertaining to humanity; it primarily applied to the transition from medieval to modern modes of thought. Humanism had its origin in the schools of the free cities to meet the growing needs of an urban society. These philosophers conceived education not to be completed at an educational institution or during childhood, but rather education was a continuous process in activities, associations and pleasures. These factors, too, they said were a part of education. The Humanists restructured the past to add to a better understanding of themselves and the time in which they lived and had their being. Renaissance Humanism dealt with the direct study, rediscovery and cultivation of Greek and Roman classics.

The intellectual and cultural revolution of Humanism was present throughout Europe; many social and educational economic reforms resulted. Close relationships existed between Italian and other European Humanists as existed among French, Dutch, English and German Humanists.

It can be said that the Humanists performed several services to education. They encouraged a new interest in the intellectual and aesthetic accomplishments of the ancients, and second, they established new schools whose emphasis was on individuals, their personal development and their self-realization. The most outstanding Italian Humanists included Petrarch, Boccaccio and Vittorino da Feltre, all born in the early fourteenth century.

Among the outstanding northern Christian Humanists was Erasmus (1466–1536), who believed God to be the primary concern of life and the center of the universe. Born in Rotterdam, Holland, he waged battle with theologians because of his superstitions although he maintained a strong faith in God. He held that education must beware of conceit because hypocrisy governed most of mankind. Erasmus advocated the careful training of teachers as seen in his *Upon the Method of Right Instruction.* He proposed independent judgment in education in which genuine knowledge and honesty were combined. Rather than using force and coercion with pupils, Erasmus believed in setting a scholarly example for them. He believed humility to be the most important attribute of a scholar.

Erasmus' *Adagio,* a collection of sayings from the writings of classical authors, is said to be the most popular of all of his writings. Among his other works are *On the Education of a Christian Prince, On Christian Matrimony* and *Colloquies.* Finally, the clerical monopoly of education and learning were destroyed by the Renaissance.

The Reformation

The Reformation, or the revolt from the Catholic Church of Rome, in the sixteenth century was connected with the Renaissance and the advocates of Humanism. The transformation brought about at this time by the religious reforms was advocated by Martin Luther, Calvin and Zwingli. The state became more important in the educational system. Countries in which the Reformation had its most profound effect were England, France, Germany, Sweden and Scotland.

Calvin played an auspicious part in the establishment of the Calvinist or "Reformed" Church, which along with the Lutheran Church were the two distinct church organizations of sixteenth-century Protestantism.

Zwingli was the leader of a contemporary movement with that of Martin Luther that appeared in Switzerland. It was Zwingli who brought the spirit of the trained scholar to the study of the Scriptures.

Martin Luther (1483–1546) advocated the education of the masses under the leadership of the citizens or civil authorities. He understood that this type of education would be in the public interest with financing by councils of citizens. Martin Luther was a social reformer; he felt those of lesser means and those who needed to work would divide their time between several hours at school and the remaining time in learning a trade. He felt that although public schools would have a limited operation time, girls as well as boys should attend.

The Reformation in Germany gave rise to the gymnasia or the higher schools. These schools were outgrowths of burgher schools, which were schools in boroughs, and the cathedral schools. By the end of the eighteenth century, elementary or lower schools called "Volkschulen" blossomed in almost all villages and towns.

The results of this massive movement were significantly far-reaching. Education at the elementary level was extended. The native or vernacular language took on a new importance, and work training made education more meaningful and disciplined. Church authorities retained control of education in the Catholic Church. Civil or citizen control of education was promoted by the Protestants together with compulsory education.

Comenius

John Amos Comenius (1592–1670), born in Monravia, Czechoslovakia, was an educational reformer in the seventeenth century. He had a philosophy that was humanitarian. Forced by circumstances brought about by the Thirty Years' War to wander from country to country— Germany, Poland, England, Sweden, Hungary, Transylvania, and Holland—deprived of his wife and children and property, he at one time reflected, "My life was one long journey. I never had a homeland."

Comenius developed and wrote the first systematic and complete treatise on education derived from psychological understanding of the learning process in children. His philosophy contained three levels which held that (1) peace on earth exists only when religious factions cease to fight and unite toward the realization of God's will; (2) such understanding and cooperation can be achieved best through universal knowledge or "pansophia" among all nations and all men achieved by (3) widespread educational reforms in methods and principles of teaching including a universal language and universal coeducation. His *Didactica* was a graded organization in the learning process which begins with infancy and continues through research institutions. Thus, school involved infancy to age six in the "mother school" or family group, seven to twelve in "vernacular school"; thirteen to eighteen, the grammar school or Latin school; and, lastly, the university, nineteen to twenty-four years of age. Beyond this four-grouping school system Comenius could visualize a "college of light," or an academy of sciences for the centralizing of all knowledge. He believed in progress through science.

The works of Comenius include *The Great Didactic, The School of Infancy, The Gates of Tongues Unlocked,* and *The Vestibule.*

John Locke

Various philosophical and societal trends of the eighteenth century had a bearing on educational thought. Several of these trends were Pietism, developed by Philipp Spencer and August Francke; the realism which originated with Ratke and Comenius and the Enlightment; and the spiritual and humanitarian movement of John Locke (1632–1704), an English philosopher.

Following the Glorious Revolution of 1688, Locke, after much work in methods of reasoning in medicine and philosophy, began to publish the results of his lifetime of philosophical thought and study. He theorized that governments are designed for the happiness and well-being of man rather than for the perpetuation of the ruling class. One of the most important thinkers of all times, Locke questioned the usefulness of classical language and rhetoric. He contended that human beings should cultivate a sound body; he stressed the importance of good physical health and a sound mind with both being dependent upon the other. Locke felt that a teacher should love children, should know and practice self-control and use reasoning in dealing with children rather than resorting to corporal punishment. Some of his works include *Essay Concerning Human Understanding, Letters Concerning Toleration* and *Two Treatises on Government.*

Rousseau and Naturalism

Following the Reformation, education became more formal; the curriculum designed to strengthen character of the students became difficult and unpleasant. Schools developed throughout Europe, but new discoveries in science retarded educational development. Christian devotion and dedication as the way to the good life were emphasized by the Pietists. This was a Protestant movement of renewed faith in the seventeenth and eighteenth centuries that encouraged individual prayer and humility. Thinkers believed the way to happiness was through clear thinking and reason. Jean Jacques Rousseau (1712–1778) offered a third answer. He contended that the only way a man could be happy was by reverting back to nature. Rousseau influenced education. He held several premises: teachers must study their students, child nature is inherently good, discipline is wrong. He further maintained in his educational theory the need for the development of independent judgment, attention to naturalness and founding a general humanity. The child, according to Rousseau, should be educated to be a man such as a priest or soldier; girls should be educated as girls in keeping with their role in life as mother or homemaker.

Although Rousseau's philosophies dealt with the upper classes, his influence was important with the masses in the spread of sciences, in the elimination of the grasp of humanism and scholasticism and in leaving a legacy of educational thought prevalent today. He is remembered for his writings; *Emile, Discourse on the Moral Effects of the Arts and Sciences, Discourse on the Origin and Foundation of Inequality Among Men* and *Confessions, The Social Contract* and *The New Heloise.*

Idealism, Its Philosophy and Influence

Among other great men who influenced modern education Pestalozzi, Froebel, Herbart, Fichte, Leibniz, Kant and Hegel may be termed idealistic philosophers, for they embraced the philosophy of idealism. Idealists profess the world to be intelligible or spiritual in its ultimate or highest form; this law-abiding universe depends upon how it is perceived by the mind. Philosophers term some idealism absolute and another kind subjective. Absolute idealism regards the external world as being existent only in the consciousness of its perceivers, while subjective idealism regards the external world as independent of the perceiver. Idealism embodies a regard for a higher and more spiritual view of life. To idealists, evil is not ultimate but is usually traced to a materialistic philosophy and is generally associated with man's lower drives or emotional cravings.

Pestalozzi

Johann Heinrich Pestalozzi (1746–1827) was a Swiss educational theorist. Through education, he tried to improve the downtrodden. His own theories were patterned after those found in Rousseau's *Emile*. He believed in developing a child from within rather than imposing adult standards upon him from without.

Pestalozzi's most important works are *Leonard and Gertrude, The Evening Hours of a Hermit, How Gertrude Teaches Her Children* and *Swan Song*. This Swiss philosopher contended that all humans possess some creativity and a capacity for love and understanding. He revamped the curriculum in the instruction in arithmetic, language and geography. He encouraged the teaching of and emphasized the need for manual training for all persons, not only for the laboring class. To him, development through the head, the hand and the heart was important. This great idealist stressed the model for the school to be the home. He desired to establish an ethical society where God would be worshiped.

Herbart and Froebel

Two European followers of Pestalozzi exerted an important influence on education. Johann Herbart (1776–1841) developed a list of procedures to assist in the orderly conduct of each educational lesson. These concepts were developed into the five formal steps in instruction which included preparation, presentation, comparison and abstraction, generalization and application. The areas of language, history and literature should be stressed.

Friedrich Froebel (1782–1852), a German educator, was a protege of Pestalozzi and known to be the father of the kindergarten. Nonetheless, Froebel's educational work was not specifically limited to small children. Among his beliefs were education without coercion, the use of self-activity, the development of creativity and the belief that children by nature are good. His greatest contribution was his kindergarten school; this contribution was his most important to European and American education.

Gottfried Leibniz

Gottfried Leibniz (1646–1716), another idealist, was a philosopher and a mathematician. He believed that God exists and he used four arguments as proof of God's existence. The first was ontological, that the concept of God necessitates existence and as a subject of perfection God must exist. Second, in the universe contingency exists that is the possibility of something happening, but it depends upon necessity. We need a cause that is necessary and that cause is God. This is known as cosmological argument. The third argument is gained from the nature of truth. Leibniz was optimistic; he believed there to be only one God. In education he stressed discipline, the teaching of Latin and history, mathematics, sciences, music, classical languages, travel and dramatics.

Immanuel Kant

Immanuel Kant (1724–1804), a philosopher of merit, based his philosophies on truth. It is transcendental, which deals with a prior knowledge of phenomena. His writings and thinking dealt with the soul. He envisioned three postulates of morality: freedom, the immortality of the soul and the concept of a future life. Kant did not approve of state education, and he felt philosophers and educators needed to combine their efforts and develop a new system of education based upon dignity of the individual and moral law. His works include *Prolegomena, To Any Future Metaphysics, Critique of Practical Reason* and *Critique of Judgment.*

Johann Gottlieb Fichte

Johann Gottlieb Fichte (1775–1814) was a philosopher, a German nationalist and an educational reformer. Fichte felt the teacher to be concerned with the development of ideas and for mankind's welfare. His *Addresses to the German Nation* advanced a new educational system embodying scholarship, discipline and state control of schools. To him, a teacher must possess the highest spiritual ideals and be the mediator between the subject matter and the student. A German, he expressed German cultural superiority in *Addresses to the People.*

George W. F. Hegel

The last of the idealists for scrutiny is George W. F. Hegel (1770–1831). His aim was to synthesize nature and man's mind. He believed the state exemplifies the ideals of God. Education's purpose, he contended, is a process of developing freedom. Among his works are *The Encyclopedia of Physical Sciences, Phenomenology of the Spirit, Philosophy of Religion, History of Philosophy* and *Science of Logic.* The teacher, Hegel submitted, was to help the student develop his powers of learning and thought and to understand concepts that are universal; the teacher must use types of discipline when students need to be reminded to exhibit self-control; and he must be an interpreter of the ways of the world.

5

Education: The Institution
and Its Proponents

Numerous philosophies, movements, revolutions, group actions, social conditions and changes and individual action in countries throughout the world commanded a significant bearing on educational thought and practices to come. From the Middle Ages on, supernatural beliefs about the world, its creativity and thought have been superseded by man's considerations with this life.

Changes were noted in religious thinking and in scientific and educational exploration. Agnosticism was a result of the decay of the unity which was present in medieval times. Agnosticism is one of the movements which has affected educational thought. It is the doctrine or teaching that affirms that neither the existence or the nature of God nor the origin of the universe is known, that all knowledge is relative, thus uncertain.

Various movements and people influenced religious thinking and encouraged agnostic thinking. The Glorious Revolution, with Locke as its leader, advocated religious tolerance, which aided the Jews and the Catholics who had suffered discrimination; the French Revolution was directed against social privilege and thus restrained the church's influence, resulting in secular education as opposed to religious education. In America, Adams, Paine, Jefferson and the liberators of the American Revolution were opposed to traditional religious toleration, and as a result of their work the separation of the church and the State was affected, thereby giving a quiet impetus to the development of American education.

In the theory of evolution of Charles Darwin one sees inferences that man evolved from lower forms of life and that historical facts could not be subordinated in religious beliefs. Since Darwin's theory held no validity to the belief of God's creation of man, to God's being the alpha and the omega of life, agnosticism was encouraged. Some of its exponents were Comte, who believed man could be enlightened by science;

Hume, who believed in the obsolescence of the educational curriculum
of his time; Mill, who believed in self-development of students; Spencer,
who had no liking for the church and was also a critic of religion; and
finally, Huxley, who believed as the agnostics, who neither denied nor
affirmed the existence of God and that nature must be controlled
through science. Education, said Huxley, can only aid in man's growth
when it becomes a practical way of life.

Other ideals synonymous with various cultures have been instrumental in bringing about changes in education and educational thought.
Gandhi's strong faith, high ideals, and steadfast love for his people have
given Western civilization ideas to cultivate in education as we work to
improve and develop youth in the educative process.

Tolstoy held ideas worthy of note. He theorized that children should
be taught to place love for mankind above civilization, nation and race,
that the warm personality of a teacher is important in education and that
all mankind needs education—adults as well as children.

Education entails many facets in its development and growth because
of the complexity of the many areas involved in its implementation and
due to the numerous institutions of learning and the educational exponents who assume the responsibility of its fulfillment. It is an impossibility to contain in one book a complete educational appraisal; thus
herein we are prevailing upon those aspects which seem pertinent and
close to those who believe in its fundamental good, in the furtherance of
its sound development and in the fostering, improvement and preserva-
tion of the American democratic way of life.

Education in the United States

A number of educational ideas concerning learning were brought to
America by the early settlers from Europe. They hoped these ideas
would be inculcated in American educational practice and thought.
Influenced by the religious thinking of the Reformation and the humanist
tradition of the Renaissance, the New England colonists attempted to
emulate or follow as closely as possible the European schools of education. Frontier learning was slow since making a living itself was a
struggle under frontier conditions. To insure the proper and continuous
education of their children, which they knew was important for their
survival, the early settlers did not hesitate to establish schools as hastily
as possible. Little formal education as we know it today was received by
most children. Most of their education came from home, work, church
and the community. During this early time, the educational emphasis for
establishing schools was to provide the children with religious instruc-

tion primarily in reading the Bible. Frontier life was difficult, thus little time was left for learning.

The religious beliefs, work habits and principles of character training were reflected in the schools. Higher education as well as education in the lower schools concerned the colonists. The curriculum of the Renaissance with its emphasis on mathematics and classical language was used for both liberal study and vocational preparation. As the process of American educational development became more complex, religious orthodoxy and traditional practices were questioned.

Benjamin Franklin wanted change in schools and as early as 1749 proposed an academy or secondary school in Philadelphia. In his curriculum he advocated practical skills such as surveying, navigation and preparation for careers in the professions and in business. He felt the curriculum should be relevant to the needs of life.

Several of the founding fathers professed a strong belief in the importance of public education, but it was Thomas Jefferson who translated his beliefs into reality. He suggested that educational opportunities for the common people should be a requirement of a republican government. In 1779 he offered a plan to Virginia's lawmakers for educating at public cost school children for three years. This plan was rejected, and Jefferson submitted another proposal forty years later, and again his second plan was rejected. One of his dreams materialized, however, that of the University of Virginia which opened in 1885. This school tried to combine the classics and humanities with scientific instruction.

As a result of the Ordinance of 1787 under the Articles of Confederation, a reserved area of land in each prospective township was set aside for education and support. These land grants were situated in the states of the Ohio Valley and the Great Lakes. In 1862 under the Morrill Act, every state establishing an agricultural college was granted 30,000 acres of public land.

Horace Mann, just as Jefferson, believed in education. He advocated religious freedom and better schools. He succeeded in carrying through in the legislature of Massachusetts a state board of education and thus brought about an educational regeneration. As a result of his work in Massachusetts, the appropriation of monies for schools practically doubled, teacher work was upgraded, teachers' salaries improved and many other modifications in education were made because of his thrust.

John Dewey, American philosopher and educator, developed the philosophy of instrumentalism, which has as its emphasis intelligence, universal democratization and the scientific method. These areas may be applied in education, science, art, religion, logic, psychology and in social and economic relations. William James influenced Dewey and led him to see that the old type of education was obsolete. Dewey is remembered for the following educational principles: (1) education to be inclusive as the transmission of culture and schooling is only one method of education; (2) education is not only preparation for the future, but a process of directing present experiences for accessibility to future experiences; (3) the best way to learn is by doing; (4) growth is the end of the educational process; (5) through education, individual growth may be stimulated since individuals differ from one another; (6) directed activity, experiment and investigation should supplant mechanical drill and (7) the spirit of the classroom should be that of a group of individuals cooperating together.

Among Dewey's works are *How We Think, Democracy and Education, The School and Society, Problems of Men* and *The Knowing of the Known.*

Black Americans Who Influenced Education

Frederick Douglass

Frederick Douglass (1817–1895) was born in Easton, Maryland, of a Negro slave mother and a Caucasian father. This great orator and journalist was brought up on the plantation of his birth where he lived until he was ten years old. After teaching himself to read and write, he escaped in 1838 from the home of a Baltimore shipbuilder who had bought him. He eluded his master and authorities in the disguise of a sailor, under the name of Douglass.

While in New Bedford, Massachusetts, working for a time as a day laborer, he married a Negro woman. Because of his outstanding oratorical abilities, he was employed by the Massachusetts Antislavery Society where he was a powerful lecturer. This success on the platform led to engagements for him in England. It was during this time, when he remained in England two years, that he wrote his autobiography and that a $600 donation helped him acquire his freedom. He moved to Rochester, New York, where during the Civil War he encouraged blacks to enlist in the army and from 1847 to 1860, he published an antislavery paper.

Other great honors eventually came to Frederick Douglass. He was appointed secretary to the San Domingo Commission in 1871; became presidential elector from the state of New York in 1872; and served as marshal of the District of Columbia from 1876 to 1881. In this same district, he held the office of recorder of deeds from 1881 to 1886 and was minister to Haiti from 1889 to 1891.

This great orator, journalist and public servant serves as a role model for youths, and his illustrious career points up the fact that youths of color may not only aspire to high political offices, but they also may realize the fulfillment of their ambitions. Numerous public schools, public buildings, institutions and organizations are named in honor of this renowned American, Frederick Douglass.

Booker T. Washington

Booker T. Washington (1858–1915) was born in slavery on the Virginia plantation of an illiterate mother and a Caucasian father. He overcame the odds of poverty and deprivation to become a leader in education and an exponent of industrial education's place in education. A graduate of Hampton Institute in Virginia, he took on menial jobs to accomplish his dream of completing college.

He was called to teach at Tuskegee Institute, Alabama, a school for blacks founded through the efforts of Lewis Adams, a white man. Lewis Adams influenced the state legislature to appropriate $2,000 for the school to create a strong black vote in Adams's favor.

Booker T. Washington found the school to be only a run-down plantation housing a stable and a henhouse. Being the sole teacher, he opened the school in the two buildings with thirty students and no funds to make improvements. Working against the odds of lack of funds (the $2,000 had been voted for teachers' salaries), the hostility of whites against education for blacks and his advocacy of agriculture, he worked tirelessly until in 1901, on the anniversary of its twentieth year, Tuskegee had a staff of 110 officers and instructors and 1,400 students with some of them from South America, Africa, Cuba, Puerto Rico and Jamaica. The school owned at this time 66 buildings; 30 industrial departments; 2,300 acres of land, 1,000 under cultivation by students, representing a total value of $1,700,000. As an exponent of industrial education, Booker T. Washington taught many young people to earn a living in a definite way, thus earning a distinguished place as an immortal of education. He was elected to the American Hall of Fame in 1945.

William E. B. DuBois

Dr. William Edward Burghardt Du Bois (1868–1963) was a graduate of Fisk University where he received his M.A. and Harvard University where he was granted a Ph.D. He is the first black American to write books of a distinguished caliber and scholarly merit. An outspoken foe of lynching and mob rule in America, with William Monroe Trotter, he founded the Niagara Movement, a movement which demanded full citizenship of blacks. Although no significant action resulted from this movement, it was the forerunner of another movement or organization which has been of importance in the Negro's fight for justice, the National Association for the Advancement of Colored People. Du Bois became the editor of its official magazine, *The Crisis*.

Among the works which exemplify the reputation of Du Bois as a writer of the first rank are *Color and Democracy, The American Negro Family, Gift of Black Folk, Then and Now, Dusk of Dawn* and *The Quest of the Silver Fleece.*

Dr. Ralph Johnson Bunche

Dr. Ralph Johnson Bunche (1904–1971), United Nations Peacemaker as he was called, retains a coveted place in American education, for he became a role model for black youth in particular and all people in general to emulate and was placed among the outstanding personages in history. His career as a diplomat boasts many firsts. He became the first black to hold a vitally significant position in the U.S. State Department and as one of the founders of the United Nations. He became the first American appointed Undersecretary to the U.N.

As the first head of the United Nations peacekeeping force throughout the world, he was the first man to persuade the Arabs to sit at the negotiating table with the Israelis. After being distinguished as mediator and peacemaker, he became the first black man in history to become the recipient of the Nobel Peace Prize.

In the last speech he ever made, which was delivered at the East-West Philosophers' Conference at the University of Hawaii, his conclusion was eloquently spoken as a plea for all mankind, and it proved to be one of the most far-reaching philosophical and educational lessons of all time:

> It follows that only the goal of integration makes practical sense. White men, whether in the United States and the United Kingdom, or in the minority as in South Africa, Southern Rhodesia, and the world at large, must find a way, if such there is, to purge themselves completely of racism or face an ultimate fateful confrontation of the races which will shake the very foundations of civilization, and, indeed threaten its continued existence and that of most of mankind as well.

James Weldon Johnson

James Weldon Johnson (1871–1938) was born in Jacksonville, Florida, and graduated from Atlanta University in 1894. An elementary school principal, he later studied law and was the first black to pass the Florida bar examination. In collaboration with his brother, John, in 1900 he wrote the favorite hymn of blacks, "Lift Every Voice and Sing." His brother wrote the music to this hymn. While serving as a consul in

Venezuela at the appointment of Pres. Theodore Roosevelt, Johnson published *The Autobiography of an Ex Colored Man*. This educator, poet and author believed that the production of literature was a necessary component of a race's greatness. In collaboration with his brother, he edited several books of Negro spirituals. A literary writer as well, he wrote *God's Trombone* and an autobiography, *Along This Way*, which was the last of his publications.

Carter G. Woodson

Carter G. Woodson (1875–1950), because of his writing and scholastic achievements, has become known as the "Father of Black History." Born in Virginia in 1875, he served as dean of the school of liberal arts at Howard University and later as dean of West Virginia State College, resigning in 1922 to perform black history research.

To promote historical research and writing, to publish books on Negro life and history, to promote Negro history through schools, churches, fraternal groups, homes and for the collection of historical material relative to blacks, Carter Woodson organized the Association for the Study of Negro Life and History in Chicago. The name of this educational and historical association as it is known today is the Association for the Study of Afro-American Life and History. He is known, then, as the founder of Negro History Week, which is celebrated each year in the month of February.

Mary McLeod Bethune

Mary McLeod Bethune (1875–1955) was born in Mayesville, South Carolina; her story is one revealing the difficulty of a poor black woman, one of seventeen children of slave parents, overcoming tremendous odds in order to gain an education. Her parents were sharecroppers, so any aid that she could get for educational purposes was due to her insatiable desire to achieve. Educated in a mission school and later working in a mission, Mary Bethune saw a great need for educating children of black laborers. She started her own school in Daytona which later became Bethune-Cookman College, a coeducational college where she became its president. She held other positions, including president, in the National Association of Colored Women's Clubs, Florida State Federation of Colored Women and Florida State Teachers Association of Teachers in Colored Schools.

Mary McLeod Bethune received the Spingarn Medal for her contributions to education. Her list of credentials continued and included the founding of the National Council of Negro Women in 1935. She was appointed by four presidents—Calvin Coolidge, Herbert Hoover, Franklin D. Roosevelt and Harry Truman—to various governmental positions. A model also for blacks, she was the first black woman to head a federal agency. From 1935 to 1944 she served as President Roosevelt's Special Advisor on Minority Affairs and from 1936 to 1944 was the director of the Division of Negro Affairs of the National Youth Administration.

Charles Harris Wesley

Dr. Charles Harris Wesley (1891–   ), born in Louisville, Kentucky, was prominent in establishing the field of Afro-American studies. He received his education at Fisk, Howard, Harvard and Yale universities. He received meritorious awards for his outstanding achievements to continue studies at Yale and Harvard and was awarded a Guggenheim Fellowship (1930–1931). Dr. Wesley was professor and dean at Howard University and the president of Central State in Ohio in 1942. He continues to be one of the major American Negro historians writing in the United States. A prolific writer on Afro-American history, Charles Wesley is the author of a number of books; among the books he has written are: *Neglected History*, 1965; *In Freedom's Footsteps*, 1968; *The Quest for Equality*, 1968; *Richard Allen, Apostle of Freedom*, 1935; *The History of Alpha Phi Alpha*, 1929; and *The Negro in the Americas*, 1940. An educator, historian and writer of great magnitude, he, too, serves as a role model for students.

Dr. Martin Luther King, Jr.

Dr. Martin Luther King, Jr. (1929–1968) was born in Atlanta, Georgia, on January 15, 1929. His name was Michail Luther King, Jr., until he was six years old. His father changed both their names legally to Martin in honor of the German religious leader, Martin Luther. King's father and his mother's father were both Baptist ministers. Martin Luther King, Jr., became a minister in 1947. He completed his undergraduate work at Morehouse College in Atlanta, Georgia, and received the Bachelor of Divinity degree at Crozer Theological Seminary and the Doctor of Philosophy degree at Boston University. Dr. King married Coretta Scott of Marion, Alabama, and became the pastor of Dexter Avenue Baptist Church in Montgomery, Alabama, in 1954.

Baptist minister, Civil Rights leader and exponent of nonviolence in the struggle for Civil Rights for blacks, Dr. King was awarded the Nobel Peace Prize in 1964 and was assassinated April 4, 1968, in Memphis, Tennessee. So great was his influence and impact upon Civil Rights and world peace that a national holiday will be observed in his honor on his birthday, beginning in January, 1986.

Dr. King felt that to be educated was one of the fundamental values of the rights pertinent to and aligned with American citizenship and belonged to all regardless of race. These values have been shared in by whites more than by blacks and with less added obstacles and negative attachments. Economic factors, discrimination because of race and ethnic background have been traditionally historical impediments to a well-educated minority. Apathy, resentment and the inability to find employment have all stifled the normal incentives of tens of thousands of black boys and girls. Also, the poor quality of public education for nonwhites has been reason for their educational lag. From 1896 until 1954, the "separate" but equal doctrine enunciated in *Plessy vs. Ferguson* was the controlling philosophy regulating facilities in education for blacks throughout the South and in many border states as well.

In 1954 the Supreme Court overturned the doctrine in a momentous decision signaling the end of legal segregation in public schools and by extension in all other public facilities. The historic *Brown vs. the Board of Education of Topeka* hailed the beginning of the movement toward an integrated system in the South and in the North.

Mrs. Rosa Parks's refusal to give up her seat on a Montgomery bus in December of 1955 triggered a campaign for dignity of blacks in the South and brought into focus Dr. Martin Luther King, Jr., and the Montgomery Improvement Association. Dr. King and the Rev. Ralph Abernathy provided leadership for an effective boycott against Montgomery's "Jim Crow" city bus system. In December, 1956, Montgomery desegregated its entire public transportation system.

In 1957 Dr. King and other church members formed the Southern Christian Leadership Conference designed to continue the fight against segregation. The philosophy of the SCLC was nonviolence, and Dr. King symbolized more than any other American the courage, power, integrity and efficacy of the nonviolent philosophy. Dr. King's concern for his nonviolent strategy and social justice was rooted in his Christian theology and ethics, a deeply personal religious faith including a firm belief in a personal God and in the influence of Mahatma Gandhi. Other of his best-known influences were Walter Rauschenbusch, Reinhold Neibahr and Edgar S. Brightman.

In Dr. Martin Luther King, Jr.'s view, three alternatives were open to an oppressed people: resignation, violence and nonviolent resistance. A vast wave of militancy reverberated across the United States in 1963 as the Civil Rights movement gained momentum. In a twelve-week period, 1,412 separate Civil Rights demonstrations took place, and Dr. King led demonstrations in Birmingham in what he called "the most thoroughly segregated city in the United States." So sweeping and intense was the violence that President Kennedy asked Congress to enact a sweeping

Civil Rights Act (1964), whose aim was to alleviate the blacks legalized second-class citizenship for all time.

Today, Dr. Martin Luther King, Jr., will be remembered as a role model for people of all nations and creeds as the black man's liberator, emancipator and triumphant leader as he himself voiced the aspirations and dreams long held by all black Americans:

> I have a dream that one day, on the red hills of Georgia, sons of former slaves and the sons of former slaveowners will be able to sit down together at the table of brotherhood.
>
> I have a dream that one day even the state of Mississippi, a state swelter- ing with the heat of injustice, sweltering with the heat of oppression will be transformed into an oasis of freedom and justice.
>
> I have a dream that my little children will one day live in a nation where they will not be judged by the color of their skin but by the content of their character. . .

> Copyright © 1963 by Martin Luther King, Jr. *I Have a Dream*
> Reprinted by permission of Joan Davis

Rev. Jesse L. Jackson

The Reverend Jesse L. Jackson (1942–   ) was born in 1942 and is referred to in the January, 1977, issue of *Phi Delta Kappan* (educational publication) as "Black Moses." Robert W. Cole, managing editor of *Phi Delta Kappan* states in the same issue:

> A civil rights activist in the sixties and a disciple of Martin Luther King, the Reverend Jesse L. Jackson today leads the nation's most effective movement for the fulfillment of the dreams of young inner-city blacks. The movement begins with education. Its goals will be realized, Jackson insists, only through student self-discipline and the work ethic.

The Reverend Jackson, although young in comparison to the previous black contributors to education, is included here because of his dynamic push for education and economic justice for blacks. Young people look up to him as a liberator and emancipator—a deliverer from the fetters of inequity and disillusionment that continue to bind them.

Jesse Jackson, a 1984 candidate for President of the United States, the second black in history (Shirley Chisholm, the first), is president of Operation PUSH (People United to Save Humanity) and the founder of EXCEL the PUSH Program for Excellence in Education, the movement for the upgrading in intelligence and ambition of young inner-city blacks. Topping the list of most influential, most popular and most admired black leaders in the United States as shown in polls taken by magazines and newspapers, Jesse Jackson has become a well-known fighter for inspiring young blacks, for expanding economic opportunities and in challenging white-owned businesses to hire blacks; he works with zeal for the elevation of the disenfranchised. A graduate of North Carolina A & T College, he was a veteran in the nonviolent movement of Dr. Martin Luther King. An outspoken advocate for social justice and equal opportunity in employment, he joined CORE and later the SCLC (Southern Christian Leadership Conference). Later, at the direction of Dr. Martin Luther King, he headed Operation Breadbasket, the economic arm of the SCLC. A man of articulate ability and intellectual acumen, his communication skills reveal an innate and astute capacity and adeptness in discussing with keenness and accuracy many issues of social and political concern.

PUSH, an outgrowth of Operation Breadbasket, has as its aim since its inception on Christmas Day, 1971, the development of black economic and political strength with emphasis on four major areas, which include voter registration, education, economic development and international development.

The Rev. Jesse Jackson was instrumental in the release of a twenty-seven-year-old American aviator, Lt. Robert O. Goodman, Jr., a navigator bombadier on an A-6E Intruder jet which was shot down December 4, 1983, during an American air strike against Syrian antiaircraft positions in Lebanon. His pilot was killed in the raid, which was in retaliation for attacks on U.S. reconnaissance flights, and Lieutenant Goodman was captured and held prisoner.

The Reverend Mr. Jackson traveled to Damascus, Syria; he met with President Hafez Assad and made a direct appeal for Lieutenant Goodman's release. As a result of Jesse Jackson's efforts, Lieutenant Goodman was released January 3, 1984, approximately one month after the Lieutenant's incarceration.

The Reverend Mr. Jackson refuted the inference that he engaged in the mission because of race; Lieutenant Goodman is black. Pentagon officials sent a U.S. military plane to bring Lieutenant Goodman home. Also, on the flight was the Reverend Mr. Jackson, who was lauded by President Reagan, the press, television and the nation for his heroic personal mission in the interest of humanity.

Because of the Reverend Mr. Jackson's push for excellence in education, for his dedication to the regeneration of a downtrodden race, and for his humanitarian spirit, he is included here as a role model for students to emulate and as a champion of Civil Rights. Thus, the Rev. Jesse Jackson is, perhaps, the most outstanding, charismatic, most outspoken and influential black civil and human rights leader today as he continues to exhort unmitigatedly to black youth to believe they are "somebody."

6

Periods of Educational Growth in the United States

Four periods of historical development mark the growth of education in the United States. As indicated previously the first period is identified with the early settlers' transplantation of European types of institutions and may be designated from 1640 onward. Each period of development was brought about as a reaction to needs, to social demands and democratic ideals. Because of a dearth of immigrants to this country, an increase in wealth and materialism and the change to a democracy from an aristocracy, there was a decline in emphasis during the second period from the middle of the eighteenth century to approximately 1830. From 1830 to 1890, the third period gleaned industrial growth, the incorporation of municipalities and an influx of people into the country. The fourth period is the present twentieth century in which environmental, political, social and technological changes have brought about noticeable alterations in educational theories and practices.

Schools have been recognized since the beginning of the nation as a preservative institution of our democracy. The Continental Congress realizing these principles two months before the adoption of the Constitution, passed the Ordinance of 1787 for the government for territory northwest of the Ohio River. This document recognized for the first time in unified form the democratic ideal of the government's responsibility to man. This ordinance stated that: "Religion, morality and knowledge being necessary to good government and the happiness of mankind, schools and the means of education shall forever be encouraged." This ordinance proved to be a model for almost all state constitutions written as America moved forward and as territories were granted statehood and became a part of these United States.

Kindergarten

Kindergarten, which comes from the German words, "kinder" meaning children and "garten," meaning garden, is a school for young children which most enter just before the first grade in elementary school and must be five years old on or before January 1 of the year they enter as required by some school systems. The school's procedures and curriculum are based on the theory that education should begin by engendering in the child the normal tendencies or aptitudes of play, exercise, creativity, imitation, observation and construction. The kindergarten places emphasis on social training.

As early as 1860, kindergarten existed in America and as early as 1873 one was in a public school. Their theory may be traced to the work of Friedrich Froebel, a German educator known to be the "father of the kindergarten." He stressed the value of play in the child's early development. His work with "occupations" and "gifts" was stilted and regimented in drawing out the child's nature. Later, however, under John Dewey and Patty Smith Hill the emphasis was broadened, and eventually the theory has evolved that presumably the child develops as a result of real world experiences. This early education was referred to as child-centered education. The proponents of this child-centered approach to education advocated fitting the school to the needs of the child.

Maria Montessori, educator of Rome, was also a pioneer in the kindergarten movement. Her method assumed the necessity of the child's escape from adult domination by first changing adults' superiority attitudes toward children and providing a new environment for the child. Her ideas of self-help and accepting responsibility were valuable.

In the last two decades of the nineteenth century, kindergartens were adopted with rapidity. The Division of Kindergarten Education, Department of the Interior, was created in 1913. Today, most of the kindergartens are in the public school system and are considered an integral part of early childhood training.

Nursery Schools or Prekindergartens

The new trend in childhood education in recent years has been in preschool education, particularly education prior to kindergarten. Many youngsters today obtain valuable early training in nursery schools whether their attendance is because of their parents' employment or essentially because of the training.

In 1965, under the Elementary and Secondary Education Act, $775 million was appropriated to subsidize projects. The nursery school was a recipient of this funding. At the advent of the twentieth century there were few nursery schools; however, by 1970 this school, which is a prekindergarten school serving thousands of young children, was growing in popularity. The activities which these youngsters begin practically as soon as they learn to walk include play, learning to be neat and orderly, sharing, relating to one another and engaging in sightseeing excursions with adult supervision.

Dramatic Strides Made Later in the Nineteenth Century

The Development of the Common School

During the latter half of the nineteenth century, the nation saw gigantic changes; the steamboat and railroads came into being, commerce and agriculture flourished and the nation saw broad expansion and steady growth in land and population. This age of growth, progress and social and moral advancements brought about a new confidence and an optimism of the common man to express himself through his voting privilege and his right to hold political office.

Thus, in this environment of transformation was developed the common school. This term "common school," originally meant a school for all and was distinguished from European institutions, which were limited to certain classes of students. This common school was open to all and upheld by public funds. It was to be an institution of the people under the sovereignty or authority of the state; it was the forerunner of the American school of today. Public support was given primary schools in New England; however, at this time in the South the states did not support education but gave only a pauper education to the poor. In the middle states schools were at times public, but they were mostly parochial or benevolent in nature. Early common schools included only the first two or three grades, and the subject content was mainly the basics of reading, writing and arithmetic. Later, as educational needs and desires grew, the common school embodied the first eight grades. The common schools provided the impetus for the public high schools, and in 1821 the nation's first high school opened in Boston. The high school in the twentieth century is regarded now as a right of every American, and most educators look upon the four-year college as a part of public education.

Education in the Twentieth Century

At the opening of the twentieth century, public education is free, is compulsory and articulates from elementary to junior high school or middle school, as is the case in some states, to senior high school. Education is free, universal and compulsory although the requirements for school attendance and the amount of free schooling vary from state to state. Many students attend church-related schools and private institutions in addition to the public schools.

Early Secondary Schools

Early secondary schools catered only to those able to afford them and who were planning to attend college or enter the professions. It was in this educational backdrop of aristocracy that the public secondary schools were born to serve the common people's educational needs. Intellectual development and social responsibility were reestablished with the establishment of public high schools.

The importance of the Westward movement, urbanization and the industrial revolution pointed up a need for higher education or schooling beyond elementary grades. The need for highly trained people in industry and business and the belief in equality of opportunity as implied in the nation's democratic principles called for public schools to be open to all.

Basically education was to be equal opportunity, but even today with the desegregation of schools, equality is not yet a reality.

American education, like societal, economic, political and industrial change, has brought about a change in education. At the beginning of the present century students attended an elementary school for eight years, and those going on attended four years of high school. This was the "8-4" plan. Later, there appeared the 6-3-3 plan, which included six years of elementary study and three each in the junior and senior high schools.

The high schools have become more realistic and are offering courses in preparation for what most of the students may pursue as a livelihood or as homemakers, particularly since those who do not attend college are in the majority. Among them are courses in the areas of nursing, woodwork, dramatics, writing, secretarial training, shop courses and driver education. In addition, there are courses on the family and marriage and computer education, in which students will become acquainted with how computers are used in society, various types of equipment used in information processing, terminology of computer systems and the way to program a computer to do a specific job.

At the present, several states have instituted compulsory attendance to age sixteen and some seventeen, thus high school attendance in these instances is mandatory.

Because of a decline in enrollment in junior and senior high schools, as some educators say, there has come about a change in grade plans in some districts. The junior high school has become a middle school with grades six through eight, and in some systems grades five through eight, while grade nine has been incorporated in the high schools, thus, a 5-3-4 plan or a 4-4-4 plan has been developed. Among other reasons for the change to the middle school is that these adolescents need to be in this particular setting because of the similarities of needs of this age group involving social maturation, learning abilities and problems and concerns significant to their level. Due to the change in subject matter, teacher certification and preparation, the need for a well-defined guidance program and in-service programs is mandatory.

Numerous social problems including drugs, alcohol, suicides, and truancy pose an urgent need for changes and alterations in organization. Many universities and organizational specialists offer workshop materials for in-service programs for middle schools. Various state education departments, school systems and local education associations also offer effective in-service programs. While preservice training for middle school teachers is at a low ebb, it is certain that colleges and universities in the very near future will incorporate such plans in their teacher training programs. Many outstanding books, periodicals and bulletins by contemporaries in education are available on middle school teaching, subject matter and students. Among them are *The Handbook for Middle School Teaching* by Paul George and Gordon Lawrence (Scott, Foresman 1982) and *The Exemplary Middle School* by William Alexander and Paul George (Holt, Rinehart & Winston, 1981). Periodicals containing information pertinent to the middle schools are *The Middle School Journal of Early Adolescence* and the *Bulletin of the National Association of Secondary School Principals,* 1983 issue.

Colleges and Universities in America

Colleges and universities are institutions of higher learning. Generally the term "college," which in its Roman context, was any association of persons organized for a specific purpose such as politics or religion. The distinction between a college and university is somewhat vague and often the words are used interchangeably. Generally a college includes all institutions of higher learning. On the other hand, universities encompass institutions having several departments or professional schools. Often the university has several branches which may be on the same or different campuses.

.The earliest universities in the United States were founded basically upon religious ideals as evidenced in the early ones like Harvard, the oldest and best-known university, founded in 1636 by Congregationalists; William and Mary, aided in its establishment by the Episcopalians; Princeton, begun by the Presbyterians; while Brown University was established by the Baptists.

The University of Pennsylvania, established in 1755, was the first nonsectarian university. Here various religious beliefs were tolerated. Ecclesiastical control of universities during the eighteenth century was the cause of much rebellion among universities. However, today most major universities are nonsectarian or not directed by any religious group or sect.

The colleges of Scotland and England were the patterns for the organization of early universities. The influence of the German universities, particularly in the nineteenth century, was clearly evident.

The impetus to the spread of higher education stemmed from national legislation, as seen in the provision of the Northwest Ordinance of 1787. Under its provisions land was sold to the Ohio Company with sections set aside for the support of universities. Benefiting by this legislation was Ohio University, established in 1803. The federal government since that time has given many thousands of acres to the states for the support of higher education. State universities have become a significant part of American education and many rival private and sectarian institutions in scholastic superiority and educational propensity.

Oberlin College in 1833 introduced coeducation, thereby aiding the development of the university in America. Various colleges for women have been opened, such as Mount Holyoke in 1931. Since that time other women's colleges have opened including Sarah Lawrence, Vassar and Smith. Some universities formerly for men or women exclusively have opened their doors to the opposite sex, becoming coeducational centers of learning.

Among the early universities for blacks were Atlanta University, Atlanta, Georgia, founded in 1865; Lincoln University, Jefferson City, Missouri, 1866; and Hampton Institute, Hampton, Virginia, in 1868.

By the passage of the Morrill Act, the federal government aided the development of agricultural colleges. Every state under this act created a separate university or unified an agricultural and mechanical arts college with another institution. Some of these institutions, like Texas A & M, offered liberal arts training together with vocational and mechanical arts education.

Junior Colleges and Community Colleges

There are also in many states or local communities two-year junior colleges or community colleges. These colleges provide vocational and liberal arts professional training or serve as two-year programs for college or university entrance.

The first of the public junior colleges was established in 1902 in Joliet, Illinois. Since that time junior colleges have flourished throughout the nation. A national organization of the junior colleges was organized in 1920 and it was the American Association of Junior Colleges. The *Junior College Journal* is the official publication of this organization. Foundations like the Carnegie Foundation and the Rockefeller Foundation have aided the program of the junior colleges and in determining their purpose in the field of higher education through special grants.

A decision of the North Carolina Court in 1930 guaranteed public tax support of the junior college. A North Carolinian had questioned the right of Asheville, North Carolina, to levy taxes for junior college support. The court held that the principles applying to the support of the junior college were the same as that for the high schools.

7

The Uniqueness of Education in the United States

The uniqueness of the educational system in the United States exists because there is no national system of education. This is unlike the education in many countries where national systems exist and where centralized controls are geographically strategic and practical, such as in various Middle Eastern countries like Turkey and Egypt. The United States' educational system involves local control on state, county and community levels. There exists in the country, in addition to the state public school systems, church affiliated administered schools such as parochial schools and a diverse group of privately supported schools.

The government has an agency in educational affairs in the United States, the Office of Education, which was established by Congress in 1867. It was transferred in 1939 from the Department of the Interior to the Federal Security Agency. In 1953 the U.S. Office of Education became a branch of the Department of Health, Education and Welfare. The function of this agency is for the collection, interpretation, publication and dissemination of information concerning education in this country and other countries.

The Office of Education has been in charge of various projects promoted by the federal government, such as conducting educational research, exchange programs in which students and teachers exchange study with other countries, various vocational education programs, particular areas of land-grant college administration, program planning services regarding school standards of administration instruction, finance, teacher training supervision and the promotion of practices and ideas in education throughout the country. While the Office of Education is instrumental in the improvement of educational programs at all levels, it must be realized that it has no direct administrative power.

The general responsibility of education in the United States is delegated to the states. The powers and duties of the state regarding education have been dealt with before; however, various additional factors of merit and concern which affect education will be cited.

State Boards of Education

The educational administration on the state level is headed by a state board of education. Such a board may be elected, appointed by the governor or by the state legislature. The duties of a state board of education vary from state to state, but they all have as their major concerns the distribution of state or federal funds allocated to the states. The enforcement of educational statutes, the determination of basic courses of study, the recommendation or adoption of textbooks, the certification of teachers, the provision of library services, maintenance, building standards and the approval and operation of teachers' colleges are the responsibilities of the state government. State boards of education also concern themselves with the improvement of local operations, the improvement of education as a governmental function, providing educational opportunities for all and the provision of educational leadership. Specialists known as helping teachers provide classroom supervision. Local boards of education, usually elected by the people, assume the administrative authority of the schools. These boards usually have first priority in levying taxes and are independent sources of revenue usually not subject to rejection by other bodies.

Local Boards of Education

Local boards of education select the superintendent of schools, and with him rests the duty of the recommendation of school personnel for appointment to the board. The duties of this board are exerted in the interest of the needs of the community. To the local board is usually entrusted the determination of educational policies and the hiring of nonteaching personnel. Assistance is given by the board of education to the superintendent in the preparation of the budget.

There are schools for the physically and mentally handicapped, the blind, deaf, dumb, crippled and those who are mentally handicapped. Many states and cities have provided educational opportunities in the way of special programs for the handicapped. The amount of $1 million was appropriated by Congress in 1958 to assist in preparing for the teaching of the handicapped and such aid has since been increased.

Federal, state, foundation money of large private donations and gifts have brought into prominence special programs for bright students. Special programs in elementary and secondary schools for bright students include field trips, supplementary books, research and special projects.

Much federal legislation has been approved which provides support for many other types of public education programs. For example, the Elementary and Secondary Education Act provides funds for the handi-capped, children of migrant farm workers and programs for children in low income areas who are achieving below grade level in the basic skills of reading and mathematics. The Smith-Hughes Act and the George Deen Act assist the states in providing industrial vocational education and agricultural education in high schools.

Schools in the District of Columbia

The only control of schools by the federal government occurs in the District of Columbia. Three commissioners appointed by the president control the entire government of the District of Columbia. All legislation governing the District of Columbia and all monies supplied for govern-mental operation including those needed for public schools are passed by Congress. A school board appointed by the U.S. District Court in the District of Columbia is composed of nine members.

Other Federally Operated Schools

Divisions of the federal government operate schools of specific types including the United States Military Academy at West Point, the Naval Academy at Annapolis, foreign service schools, schools for FBI training and Indian schools.

Organizations to Foster and Upgrade Education

Various associations in the field of education including teachers, administrators and other school-oriented groups have been instrumental in studying problems, analyzing and fostering educational welfare, pub-lishing data and improving the status of their members. Various ones are in the interest of diverse segments, such as the American Home Econom-ics Association, while others are in the interests of educational groups. The oldest of the latter groups is the National Education Association (NEA), founded in 1857, whose aim is "to elevate the character and advance the interest of the teaching profession." This organization, with headquarters in Washington, gained momentum in the 1870s. Through a large retinue of commissions and counselors its business is carried out in

Structure of Organization of an Exemplary School District

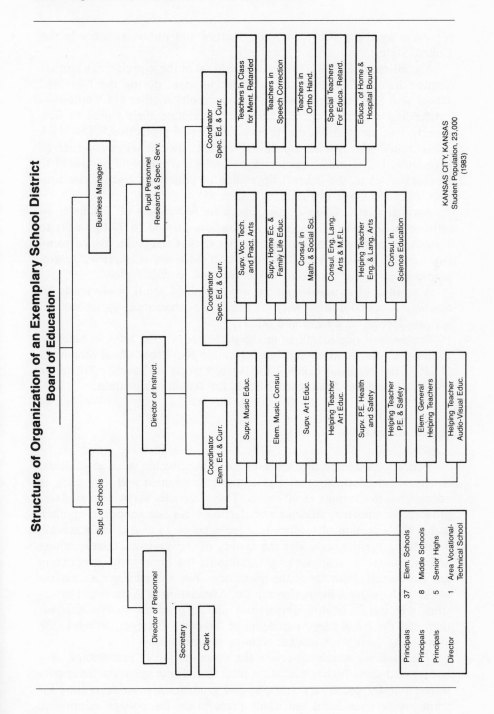

Board of Education

Supt. of Schools

Business Manager

Director of Personnel

Secretary

Clerk

Pupil Personnel Research & Spec. Serv.

Director of Instruct.

Coordinator Elem. Ed. & Curr.

- Supv. Music Educ.
- Elem. Music. Consul.
- Supv. Art Educ.
- Helping Teacher Art Educ.
- Supv. P.E. Health and Safety
- Helping Teacher P.E. & Safety
- Elem. General Helping Teachers
- Helping Teacher Audio-Visual Educ.

Coordinator Spec. Ed. & Curr.

- Supv. Voc. Tech. and Pract. Arts
- Supv. Home Ec. & Family Life Educ.
- Consul. in Math. & Social Sci.
- Consul. Eng. Lang. Arts & M.F.L.
- Helping Teacher Eng. & Lang. Arts
- Consul. in Science Education

Coordinator Spec. Ed. & Curr.

- Teachers in Class for Ment. Retarded
- Teachers in Speech Correction
- Teachers in Ortho Hand.
- Special Teachers For Educa. Retard.
- Educa. of Home & Hospital Bound

Principals	37	Elem. Schools
Principals	8	Middle Schools
Principals	5	Senior Highs
Director	1	Area Vocational-Technical School

KANSAS CITY, KANSAS
Student Population, 23,000
(1983)

representing the teachers, administrators and public schools in the United States.

According to the 1983–1984 annual edition of the association's journal entitled *Today's Education,* the association spent during the 1981–1982 school year $5.5 million—and state associations another $14.5 million— "defending members against actions that violate their rights to free speech, free association, due process, and equal protection." The NEA is concerned with teacher rights and welfare, special services—such as insurance, travel aids, legislative and political interests pertinent to teachers—and to the general upgrading of education and its constituency. (See the Code of Ethics, NEA, p. 95).

Another organization is the American Federation of Teachers, an affiliate of the AFL-CIO. This association, formed in 1916, works to better teacher conditions through teacher strikes and collective bargaining. Benefits derived from its work are in the areas of improved wages, pensions, academic freedom, sick leaves and teacher rights.

A number of national councils are organized at all grade levels for teachers in specific areas such as English, mathematics, social studies, science, foreign languages and others.

Professional organizations at the higher education level include the National Commission on Teacher Education and Professional Standards (TEPS), the National Council for Accreditation of Teacher Education (NCATE), and the American Colleges for Teacher Education.

School Accreditation

Educational accrediting agencies are of inestimable value to students, teachers and administrators and to the improvement and upgrading of educational institutions at all levels. These agencies serve as a guide to prospective students, students transferring from one school to another, and in the selection of teacher training schools. In evaluating a school, accrediting agencies consider the quality of the students, faculty rating and the status of their working conditions; the library, the curriculum and the overall character of the institution. Two accrediting associations working throughout the nation are the Association of American Universities, which is for leading universities offering graduate study accreditation, and the American Association of Teachers Colleges, which is the accrediting agency for teacher training institutions.

The agencies which supervise the accreditation of elementary, secondary and some higher education total five. These agencies are chiefly responsible for secondary schools; and graduation from accredited institutions is considered sufficient preparation for college admission.

They include the New England Association of Colleges and Secondary Schools, the Middle States Association of Colleges and Secondary Schools, the North Central Association of Colleges and Secondary Schools, the Northwest Association of Secondary and Higher Schools and the Southern Association of Colleges and Secondary Schools.

Other professional accrediting associations accredit particular departments of colleges and universities, such as the American Association of Schools of Social Work and the American Association of Collegiate Schools of Business.

CODE OF ETHICS
of the Educational Profession
ADOPTED BY THE 1975 NEA REPRESENTATIVE ASSEMBLY

Preamble

The educator, believing in the worth and dignity of each human being, recognizes the supreme importance of the pursuit of truth, devotion to excellence, and the nurture of democratic principles. Essential to these goals is the protection of freedom to learn and to teach and the guarantee of equal educational opportunity for all. The educator accepts the responsibility to adhere to the highest ethical standards.

The educator recognizes the magnitude of the responsibility inherent in the teaching process. The desire for the respect and confidence of one's colleagues, of students, of parents, and of the members of the community provides the incentive to attain and maintain the highest possible degree of ethical conduct. The Code of Ethics of the Education Profession indicates the aspiration of all educators and provides standards by which to judge conduct.

The remedies specified by the NEA and/or its affiliates for the violation of any provision of this Code shall be exclusive and no such provision shall be enforceable in any form other than one specifically designated by the NEA or its affiliates.

Principle I—Commitment to the Student

The educator strives to help each student realize his or her potential as a worthy and effective member of society. The educator therefore works to stimulate the spirit of inquiry, the acquisition of knowledge and understanding, and the thoughtful formulation of worthy goals.

In fulfillment of the obligation to the student, the educator—

1. Shall not unreasonably restrain the student from independent action in the pursuit of learning.
2. Shall not unreasonably deny the student access to varying points of view.
3. Shall not deliberately suppress or distort subject matter relevant to the student's progress.

4. Shall make reasonable effort to protect the student from conditions harmful to learning or to health and safety.
5. Shall not intentionally expose the student to embarrassment or disparagement.
6. Shall not on the basis of race, color, creed, sex, national origin, marital status, political or religious beliefs, family, social or cultural background, or sexual orientation, unfairly:
   a. Exclude any student from participation in any program;
   b. Deny benefits to any student;
   c. Grant any advantage to any student.
7. Shall not use professional relationships with students for private advantage.
8. Shall not disclose information about students obtained in the course of professional service, unless disclosure serves a compelling professional purpose or is required by law.

Principle II—Commitment to the Profession

The education profession is vested by the public with a trust and responsibility requiring the highest ideals of professional service.

In the belief that the quality of the sevices of the education profession directly influences the nation and its citizens, the educator shall exert every effort to raise professional standards, to promote a climate that encourages the exercise of professional judgment, to achieve conditions which attract persons worthy of the trust to careers in education, and to assist in preventing the practice of the profession by unqualified persons.

In fulfillment of the obligation to the profession, the educator—
1. Shall not in an application for a professional position deliberately make a false statement or fail to disclose a material fact related to competency and qualifications.
2. Shall not misrepresent his/her professional qualifications.
3. Shall not assist entry into the profession of a person known to be unqualified in respect to character, education, or other relevant attribute.
4. Shall not knowingly make a false statement concerning the qualifications of a candidate for a professional position.
5. Shall not assist a noneducator in the unauthorized practice of teaching.
6. Shall not disclose information about colleagues obtained in the course of professional service unless disclosure serves a compelling professional purpose or is required by law.
7. Shall not knowingly make false or malicious statements about a colleague.
8. Shall not accept any gratuity, gift, or favor that might impair or appear to influence professional decisions or actions.

BILL OF TEACHER RIGHTS

Preamble

We, the teachers of the United States of America, aware that a free society is dependent upon the education afforded its citizens, affirm the right to freely pursue truth and knowledge.

As an individual, the teacher is entitled to such fundamental rights as dignity, privacy, and respect.

As a citizen, the teacher is entitled to such basic constitutional rights as freedom of religion, speech, assembly, association, and political action and equal protection of the law.

In order to develop and preserve respect for the worth and dignity of human-kind, to provide a climate in which actions develop as a consequence of rational thought, and to insure intellectual freedom, we further affirm that teachers must be free to contribute fully to an educational environment which secures the freedom to teach and the freedom to learn.

Believing that certain rights of teachers derived from these fundamental freedoms must be universally recognized and respected, we proclaim this Bill of Teacher Rights.

Article I—Rights as a Professional

As a member of the teaching profession, the individual teacher has the right:

Section 1. To be licensed under professional and ethical standards estab-lished, maintained, and enforced by the profession.

Section 2. To maintain and improve one's professional competence.

Section 3. To exercise professional judgment in presenting, interpreting, and criticizing information and ideas, including controversial issues.

Section 4. To influence effectively the formulation of policies and procedures which affect one's professional services, including curriculum, teaching materials, methods of instruction, and school-community relations.

Section 5. To exercise professional judgment in the use of teaching methods and materials appropriate to the needs, interests, capacities, and the linguistic and cultural background of each student.

Section 6. To safeguard information obtained in the course of professional service.

Section 7. To work in an atmosphere conducive to learning, including the use of reasonable means to preserve the learning environment and to protect the health and safety of students, oneself, and others.

Section 8. To express publicly views on matters affecting education.

Section 9. To attend and address a governing body and be afforded access to its minutes when official action may affect one's professional concerns.

Article II—Rights as an Employee

As an employee, the individual teacher has the right:

Section 1. To seek and be fairly considered for any position commensurate with one's qualifications.

Section 2. To retain employment following entrance into the profession in the absence of a showing of just cause for dismissal or nonrenewal through fair and impartial proceedings.

Section 3. To be fully informed, in writing, of rules, regulations, terms, and conditions affecting one's employment.

Section 4. To have conditions of employment in which health, security, and property are adequately protected.

Section 5. To influence effectively the development and application of evaluation procedures.

Section 6. To have access to written evaluations, to have documents placed in one's personnel file to rebut derogatory information, and to have removed false or unfair material through a clearly defined process.

Section 7. To be free from arbitrary, capricious, or discriminatory actions affecting the terms and conditions of one's employment.

Section 8. To be advised promptly in writing of the specific reasons for any actions which might affect one's employment.

Section 9. To be afforded due process through the fair and impartial hearing of grievances, including binding arbitration as a means of resolving disputes.

Section 10. To be free from interference to form, join, or assist employee organizations, to negotiate collectively through representatives of one's own choosing, and to engage in other concerted activities for the purpose of professional negotiations or other mutual aid or protection.

Section 11. To withdraw services collectively when reasonable procedures to resolve impasse have been exhausted.

Article III—Rights as an Organization

As an individual member of an employee organization, the teacher has the right:

Section 1. To acquire membership in employee organizations based upon reasonable standards equally applied.

Section 2. To have equal opportunity to participate freely in the affairs and governance of the organization.

Section 3. To have freedom of expression, both within and outside the organization.

Section 4. To vote for organization officers, either directly or through delegate bodies, in fair elections.

Section 5. To stand for and hold office subject only to fair qualifications uniformly applied.

Section 6. To be fairly represented by the organization in all matters.

Section 7. To be provided periodic reports of the affairs and conduct of business of the organization.

Section 8. To be provided detailed and accurate financial records, audited and reported at least annually.

Section 9. To be free from arbitrary disciplinary action or threat of such action by the organization.

Section 10. To be afforded due process by the organization in a disciplinary action.

8

The School Principal
and Administrative Philosophies

Both personal characteristics—including intelligence, general knowledge, adaptability, cooperativeness, verbal facility and professional qualifications of preparation—and professional competencies—such as the ability to work well with others, teachers and the community members, the ability to get things done efficiently and the ability to make prompt and careful decisions—are essential in elementary and secondary principalships.

Leadership at the elementary level is important because these early years in the lives of young people form the foundation for growth in the fundamentals that they may be able to pursue successfully as they are faced with more difficult studies as they reach higher levels of education. This is the first introduction of authoritarianism outside the parents' home setting.

The elementary principal is the person within the school who is most accountable for the instructional program for the school. It is through the persuasive yet kind and diplomatic approach that he is instrumental in aiding teachers to provide a continuously improved instructional program for boys and girls. Many students who have no father in the home look upon the male principal as a father image.

The competent administrator is aware of the basic texts, courses of study and materials used in the building. In addition to having an educational philosophy to use as a guide, the elementary principal, as with any individual in a leadership capacity, must continue his own professional growth. He works continuously with his teachers in fostering trust, confidence, dedication to excellence and good rapport with both students and teachers. He works for the good of the students as he recognizes those activities beneficial to children and those which encourage learning. He is always alert in securing adequate teaching materials, to maintain small classes and to eliminate poor teaching.

99

Present individuals holding principalships and those discussing the principal's role in education all agree that there are a multiplicity of demands upon the principal's time, energy and ingenuity. There is much variance in the duties principals must perform. Some are mere office duties while others bear significant importance to the children and to the school. Therefore, a principal must be well organized and must set priorities on his duties and activities after understanding fully his responsibilities. The effective principal, after learning something of the abilities and capabilities of his teachers, may delegate responsibilities to those whom he feels are qualified to carry them out. Should a principal be unaware of his duties and responsibilities, he may not infrequently become a martyr to routine duties while insubordinating those of significant import to his school. He must from time to time assess his perspective by discussions with other principals, visiting other schools, visiting the classes often in his own school, keeping professionally alert by attending meetings and seminars and through participation in studies with other administrators.

In this material the principal is referred to as he, but it is thoroughly understood that both women and men are exercising effective leadership at all educational levels including the office of superintendent of schools.

Former principals and those in the field have performed numerous studies and have written much on the corrective and preventive type of work which can be improved and the practices that may be avoided. Through reading this material the principal will gain a new perspective and insights from which to view and review the various practices of principals.

Statistics have revealed that most principals spend the greater portion of their time in personnel administration, general administration and clerical services and, thus, have too little time for supervision of instruction. These supervisory responsibilities are performed in a routine manner which leaves much to be desired in supervision as we know it.

Good secondary schools require effective educational leadership. Previously, leadership at the secondary level was not a career within itself but a stepping-stone to business enterprising, college teaching, or general administration. Selectivity in the hiring of secondary leaders has not always been a priority. Various factors such as sex, seniority of tenure, family and political ties are only a few determinants too frequently accorded disproportionate importance in the selection of administrators.

Leadership does not necessarily come from the appointed leader, the principal; it may come from the school's status in the community, faculty members of long standing, supervisors, a closely knit group of instructors, even from student groups within the school and often from PTA groups or individual parents. However, the position of principal connotes a "status" position and is usually defined in the policies of the school boards, in the job expectations of the superintendent of schools, teachers and pupils.

The functions effected by the principal and the manner in which they are carried out elevate his image and his authority in the leadership capacity. The good leader must be both an executive in the management of the school and a leader because influences are brought to bear on the ideas and policies exerted upon the teachers under his guidance, upon the students, the parents and the educational program itself. Some administrators are authoritative and rule by command and power (physical, social, or economic). A new type of leader has come about—one whose leadership is based on democratic behavior and human relationships and is a promoter of democratic ideas and principles, an organizer, a promoter of group decision, not a dictator, and a promoter of group actions.

In a survey performed some years ago, more supervising principals think of themselves as supporters rather than supervising principals. The supporters followed the dictates of the central office and felt aligned to its directives. Many principals continue to fall short in performing basic functions deemed necessary in the improvement of instruction. In a yearbook of the Department of Elementary School Principals, the National Education Association listed the most common duties of elementary school principals. The duties were designated as mandatory and discretionary. Mandatory duties were those that had to be performed or be subjected to dismissal or discipline if not performed, and discretionary duties included those in which the principal used his own judgment or discretionary powers as to whether or not something should be done.

Mandatory administrative duties included:

> To be present in buildings between specified hours
> To keep certain records and accounts
> To receipt for delivered supplies
> To check school census
> To inventory equipment, books and supplies
> To check payroll list
> To report injuries to pupils and employees
> To fly the American flag

Discretionary powers included:

> To classify pupils
> To keep personnel records of pupils
> To assign teachers
> To make curriculum schedules

To conduct teachers' meetings

To allocate funds made available for building, according to budget

To obtain substitutes for teachers who are absent

To evaluate teachers' efficiency

To supervise instruction

To cooperate with juvenile court and other law enforcement agencies

To regulate or abolish activities of teachers and pupils in the building

To handle complaints of patrons

To discipline pupils

This delineation of duties was based on a sampling of published rule books of local school boards in fifty cities of over 30,000 population. Various ones of these rules are prevalent today; others have changed. In some schools vice-principals or assistant principals are responsible for disciplining pupils and also for some complaints of parents. Principals and assistant principals must work cooperatively. Substitute teachers are obtained through the central office in most districts.

Finding time to carry out supervisory duties and to carry out other rules and regulations made mandatory by laws, state and local regulations impose a difficult burden on the principal who is required to do some teaching.

In the larger high schools are found quite frequently vice-principals who have specific duties such as the activities' program, the busing of students, school discipline, the guidance program and the extracurricular program.

9

Philosophical Principles
to Guide Administrators

All principals must have a clear-cut and working philosophy to guide them in assessing the work they are doing.

1. The administrative policies necessary to enable teachers to meet the various needs of all the pupils in heterogeneous groups should be directed toward two main goals: first, to make it possible for the teacher to know the pupil better—to know his abilities, his interests and his deficiencies well enough to direct his learning experience; and, second, to provide instructional methods and materials with a range of difficulty and content commensurate with the range of abilities and interests of the instructional group.

2. The teacher's purpose is to give the learning child a clear and detailed conception of the goal toward which he is striving and convince the youngster that it is possible to attain. If the child is not convinced that he can eventually succeed, he will remain confused and frustrated.

3. One sees in a situation only what one knows. What one gains from the reading of a selection depends entirely upon what one brings to the reading in the nature of past experience.

4. The most promising administrative development in overcoming public misunderstanding is to involve more and more citizens in actual educational planning.

5. Group achievements that are accepted and praised outside the group enhance the group's pride and cohesiveness.

6. What a person can do is more important than what he knows. Our concern is not that some bit of knowledge be learned but rather that it be used well.

7. Provide each staff member with the opportunity to work to the extent of his ability.

8. Give credit where credit is due.

9. Let each staff member know in advance about changes that affect him.

10. Let each person know where he stands.

11. The task of the administrator is to provide conditions for change.

12. School administration has the responsibility of keeping the purposes of education to the fore. These purposes of education should be a guide for the administrator's policies and actions. The soundness of his judgment will depend in no small degree upon his understanding of the nature of learning, of the demands of society and of available devices for achieving them.

Principles for Administrative Leaders

1. Treat pupils and others democratically to the extent that their competence makes possible their participation in policy-making, and to the extent that they can be led to see that in participation there is a responsibility as well as an opportunity.

2. Democracy demands that each human being be dealt with by his fellows as a living, growing, potentially flowering organism, that he has a right to be a participant in decisions that stand to affect him.

3. Democratic participation connotes more than the right to be told. It connotes, in addition, the right to influence the decision.

4. All persons in the community are potentially in the purview of the administrator when the democracy criterion is under consideration—public, parents, pupils as persons in their own right and staff.

5. The principle of political democracy says bring the exercise of control as close as possible to those affected.

6. Local self-government is the great political university where the average person is trained for the civic obligations which all sooner or later must assume if we are to continue a republic. Initiative, character, a feeling that they are a part of the government and patriotism are all born of that daily contact with government which local self-government alone can furnish.

7. Justice demands the protection of the individual from rigidity of systems of procedure, rules or laws on the one hand and from arbitrariness in the exercise of administrative discretion on the other. Mistaking uniformity for justice is a common error. Justice is a corollary to the basic democratic principle of regard for personality.

8. Prudence means "curb your heart, use your head." Prudence implies the ability to regulate, to calculate, to employ skill and sagacity in the management of practical affairs, to exercise caution; to use foresight.

9. Any group of people living within easy communication distance from one another develop various group loyalties that must be taken into account in the carrying on of an educational program.

10. Experience has shown that power is a heady drug. Those having it must be made subject to checks and balances.

11. Administrators should strive to present innovations in meaningful terms, to stress their similarities to the old.

12. Authority and responsibility should be assigned in balanced amounts.

13. Stability connotes freedom from upsetting change within the system. It does not oppose change. It counsels evolution as opposed to revolution.

14. Stability demands that proposed changes be appraised in the old frame of reference as well as in the new.

Principles of Learning

1. The goal (purpose) of the learner is the most important single factor in the learning situation. Not only does it determine what is learned, when it is learned, how it is learned and—within the limits of capacity—how well it is learned, but also, to a considerable degree, the permanency of the learning and the emotional feeling accompaniment of the learning process.

2. Retention and elimination of trial responses in the process of learning take place in terms of the goals of the learner. Most learning involves a period of trial and error. The teachers' aim is to reduce as much as possible this period of provisional trials by helping the learner associate his beginning activity with the ultimate goal.

3. The learner must believe he can achieve his goal. Numerous studies have shown that praise and encouragement are more effective than criticism in securing improvement.

4. Organization is a central concept in learning. All learning is a reorganization of previous learnings; a word defined in terms of other words. All learning is dependent upon previous learning and serves as a basis for future learning.

5. The more meaningful the learning, the more likely it is to transfer. Rote learning, routine and blind rule-of-thumb procedures and empty verbalism are almost certain to give disappointing results. Where these characteristics dominate, not much learning has occurred in the first place; therefore, there is actually nothing to transfer. Transfer depends on understanding.

6. In learning one must want something, see something, do something and get something.

All school administrators must have some philosophies such as the foregoing in order to work toward educational development and supervision.

The attractiveness of principalship varies in different parts of our country. Many are teaching principals assuming both roles. Some principals do not choose to spend the rest of their lives performing duties that they feel inconsequential to their abilities. Though there are disadvantages to the job, most believe the advantages outweigh the disadvantages. Today more than before elementary principals are having more say in the selection and assignment of teachers, have a greater voice in curriculum selection, in policy-making and in textbook selection. Secondary principals long have had significant input in the selection of the teachers in their buildings.

It is important to know that the principal of necessity must be a student of education and one interested in educational advancement. He must have a deeply profound desire to improve the educational services offered to youth, and he must be a professional leader to his staff, his students and his community. The extent of his influence will be dependent upon his conception of what a principal's job is and its importance in the growth of humanity. Much of a leader's popularity is the response of the students and the impressions of him carried to their parents. However, the greatest test of his leadership is its result in the growth and efficiency of the students' learning and development, the quality of the educational program and the end result of the production of a good school.

10

Curriculum Development

Educational development has brought about dramatic changes in elementary and secondary curricula. Teaching today is more relevant and geared to the needs of young people. Contemporary life demands that there must be inculcated in the curriculum subjects that will enable students to communicate more effectively and to aid them in making acceptable career choices and developing those characteristics and skills for successful social functioning.

Young children and even middle school and junior high school children are given the opportunity to explore, to visit businesses, community facilities and other places of interest that will generate curiosity and interest in further exploration, research and learning. Special courses and laboratories are included to increase adeptness and learning in various areas where work is below standard particularly in reading and mathematics. Various ones of these programs are subsidized by the federal government and are found in both elementary and secondary schools. Such programs are found in the areas where underprivileged children may be helped. Special teacher aides have been employed in many of these schools.

Radio, television, visual aids, records, tapes, supplementary books, learning games, reference materials, computers, projectors, films, filmstrips, sound recordings, teaching machines, traveling speakers, programs and other devices and teaching aids are being used as a means of communicating and reproducing printed educational materials. Adult education classes held in most school districts make use of many of these innovations to facilitate understanding and speed of learning. Special classes in English as a Second Language have been included in elementary and secondary schools because of the influx of Hispanics, Asian-Americans, Vietnamese and other ethnic groups whose facility to speak, understand or write English is either limited or nonexistent.

Special Education

Special education programs in the schools by tradition are thought to be for the mentally handicapped only, but these special education programs are for exceptional children who deviate socially, mentally or physically from the norm enough that their programs must be modified to enable them to reach their learning potential. Authorities in the field of exceptional children contend that these children include approximately 15 percent of the school-age population. Those deviating intellectually are referred to as below normal or subnormal, mentally retarded, or intellectually limited. The children classified as the intellectual deviates are unable to keep pace with the classwork and work abilities of normal children. They are generally classified as the educable or the trainable mentally retarded. When tested by school psychologists generally those whose IQs (intelligence quotients) are between 50 and 70 can be trained intellectually to a certain level to the extent that they become academically, socially and occupationally adjusted. They are able to support themselves fully or partially when they become grown.

Children with IQs generally between 25 and 50 are termed trainable mentally retarded. They attend special schools usually apart from the regular schools and are trained to care for themselves in dressing, toileting and feeding themselves, to become adjusted in their homes and to an extent in their community and to perform various economic services as routine duties under supervision.

Gifted children are exceptional children who are intellectually superior and have been indicated on individual intelligence tests to have IQs above 125, 130 or 140 in addition to other considerations since IQ tests are not considered conclusive. These children often perform two or more years in advance of their grade level. If not given the proper motivational work and supplementary materials for advancement, some of these children can become discipline problems at times to their own detriment.

Courses for students in PSA, Personal and Social Adjustment classes, and new courses for the educable mentally handicapped (EMH) have been introduced; special audio-visual aids, new techniques and courses in homemaking and nutrition are being taught. Objectives for learning of each individual child are carefully guided, measured and reviewed periodically. Staffings by supervisors and directors are held often that these students definitely advance as far as they are capable. Important ideas and knowledge of everyday living are being given them that they will be able to live as successfully as they are able and also that they may be able to hold some type of job. It is the consensus of many educators who work with students in this special area that they be mainstreamed or placed in classes with regular students when they are ready to keep pace.

Their placement in elective courses such as art and music eliminates, to a degree, their segregation in classes with their own group and at the same time encourages their association with average children.

Day Schools and Residential Schools

Schools which are not whole schools for serving certain types of handicapped children such as the deaf or the blind are "day" schools and "residential" schools. Day schools for other particular handicapped children are available. Students live at home and are transported to and from the schools. Residential schools are live-in or twenty-four-hour facilities for handicapped children who cannot be served in their community. The most common types of residential schools are state and private for the deaf, blind and severely handicapped.

Special Helps for Students

Special help is given those having visual, hearing and speech difficulties with special therapists and specialists being employed. Most of these children attend their regular classes each day and receive the special help at regular times during the day or week. Supervisors in specific areas, school psychologists, psychiatrists and helping teachers all play a part in aiding students to master effectively the work they are expected to grasp.

Homebound Program

Children who are confined to their homes or to the hospitals for a lengthy or indefinite period are given instruction by a Homebound teacher in order that they may resume their regular class schedule upon returning to school.

Elementary Course Offerings

In the elementary grades, the curriculum includes the basic skill subjects: reading and mathematics or arithmetic, English, spelling, science, social studies, physical education and the exploratory subjects (differing in some schools), of art, home economics, industrial education and vocal music or instrumental music. The latter five courses are generally offered at the middle school or junior high school level, but art and instrumental music, in addition to physical education, are sometimes taught on a weekly or twice-weekly basis in the elementary grades.

Special Class Offerings

Courses offered in EMH (Educable Mentally Handicapped) according to the particular school district could include basic academics, unified education and individual study which offer instruction in all regular areas of study with the work suited to the level and learning ability of the individual child.

Great care is taken in planning for the implementation of programs for these students. In one school district as in some others careful attention is given to see that their plan of study, Individual Education Plan (IEP), delineating specific goals, objectives and areas of emphasis is set and carried out. Regular staffings with teachers, counselors, principals, assistant principals and specialists are held to evaluate students, assess their progress and needs and continue plans for their advancement.

Subjects for the learning disabled include corrective reading, individual study, language arts, mathematics, reading, science and social studies.

Personal and Social Adjustment (PSA) classes held in some schools include the subjects of language arts, reading and mathematics, science, social studies, individual study and Personal and Social Adjustment. Students in this class also are mainstreamed if their performance and emotional stability warrant this action.

Diagnostic and Remedial Teachers (DART) in some school districts travel from school to school at certain periods and on certain days giving students and teachers specific helps for individuals having learning difficulties. They are basically traveling disabilities teachers for the elementary grades.

The Middle School—Junior High School Curriculum

Inasmuch as some elementary schools continue to include grades five and six, courses offered to students in those grades have been given. To be considered now will be course offerings for grades seven and eight. A similar course of study would be included in junior high school with some modifications. In middle school or junior and senior high school included in the course offerings are required courses and elective courses and the addition of several special courses.

Basic studies or the communication area of reading, English, language arts and spelling is offered in grade seven; English is offered at the eighth-grade level. Other required courses in both grades are the same but at their grade level and include mathematics, science, physical education and social studies. Special courses in grade seven are English as a Second Language and accelerated mathematics. Algebra is offered in grade eight as a special course; however, math performance, the grades on special mathematics' tests and teacher recommendations are to be considered for enrollment in this class.

Elective courses which may be chosen by students are in the areas of art, home economics, industrial education and vocal and instrumental music.

Similar courses in Learning Disabilities, Emotionally Mentally Handicapped and Personal Social Adjustment are offered in grades seven and eight with increased areas of learning and study in reading and other areas. Learning disabled and EMH students may choose a certain number of units of elective subjects. Some schools encompass a six-period day, others more. Some schools include study periods; others consider them a waste of time. A student receives one credit for a subject that lasts a full year and one-half credit is received for a semester course. To complete a school year successfully, a stipulated number of credits must be earned with emphasis upon those for required courses.

The Senior High School Curriculum

Graduation requirements in high schools are fairly consistent in most schools; however, more credits are being required in many schools as a grave awareness of the importance of education has prompted questioning and widespread concern throughout the nation concerning the goals, quality, processes, structure and relevancy of education. In some schools special requirements are made. For example, in one school system in addition to earning the required amount of credits, students must complete all thirty-five objectives in a Math Competency Test which begins in upper elementary grades and must be taken by each student enrolled in regular classes during each school year until all objectives are completed successfully. Included in the test are mathematical problems basic to a fairly comprehensive grasp of the basic skills and techniques in computation and thought processes. In order to graduate from high school a student must pass all thirty-five objectives.

The following requirements indicate what is required for graduation in a typical high school. Students are aware of the requirements early and may act accordingly as they work toward graduation. In this high school, as in some others, the mathematics class in which a student enrolls is dependent upon the number of math objectives passed by the student, or the extent of his mathematical ability. Requirements for graduation increased over a two-year period.

EXAMPLE OF HIGH SCHOOL ENROLLMENT OFFERINGS IN MATHEMATICS WHERE PASSING 35 MATHEMATICS' OBJECTIVES IS A PREREQUISITE FOR GRADUATION

Mathematics Enrollment

The following is a guide to be used for enrollment into the various Math courses. Exceptions to course enrollment must be approved by a counselor based on recommendations from your math teacher.

The number of Math Competency objectives shown should represent the number of objectives you have passed at the time of enrollment. Course sequence is to be followed (See page 113).

HIGH SCHOOL
ENROLLMENT BULLETIN
Graduation Requirement for the Classes of 1984 and 1985

1. A total of 18 credits must be earned in Grades 9 thru 12.
2. A total of 14 credits must be earned in Grades 10 thru 12.
3. LAB SCIENCE: One (1) credit in Grade 10.
4. MATHEMATICS: One (1) credit in Grade 10, 11 or 12.
   (Students graduating after May, 1980, must complete successfully before they will be eligible to receive a diploma.)
5. AMERICAN HISTORY: One (1) credit in Grade 11.
6. AMERICAN GOVERNMENT: One-half (1/2) credit in Grade 12.
7. ENGLISH LANGUAGE ARTS: Two (2) credits in Grades 10, 11 or 12.
   (All students will be continuously enrolled in an English Language Arts course while in attendance at this high school. One (1) credit of English must be earned in the 12th Grade to be eligible for graduation.)
8. Senior (Grade 12) students must enroll in and complete satisfactorily a minimum of five (5) full units of study to be certified for graduation.
9. EARLY GRADUATION: To be eligible for early graduation, students must be enrolled in six (6) subjects their senior year and earn 18 credits by the semester. Two half (1/2) credit English courses and American Government will be included, plus successful completion of the Math objectives. Careful attention will be given to past grades, attendance record and good citizenship. A principal/student con-

10th GRADE

0–15 Objectives
Fundamentals of Math

16–20 Objectives
Fund. of Math/
Intro. Algebra

21–24 Objectives
Intro. Algebra/
Geometry

25–35 Objectives
Algebra I
Geometry
Algebra II
Intro. Alg./Geometry

11TH GRADE

0–19 Objectives
Competency Math

20–24 Objectives
Competency Math/Intro. Alg.
Competency Math/Cons. Math
Intro. Alg./Geometry

25–35 Objectives
Cons. Math/App. of Cons. Math
Algebra I
Geometry
Algebra II
Math Analy./Trig.
Intro. Alg./Geometry

12TH GRADE

0–24 Objectives
Competency Math

25–30 Objectives
Competency Math
Cons. Math/Comp. Math
Intro. Alg./Comp. Math

31–35 Objectives
Cons. Math/App. of Cons. Math
Cons. Math/Comp. Math
Algebra I
Geometry
Algebra II
Math Analy./Trig.
Analytical Geom. & Calculus
Intro. Alg./Geometry

ference is required before enrollment is started. Students interested in this program should see their counselor for an application.*

Graduation Requirements for the Classes of 1986 and 1987

1. A total of 20 credits must be earned in Grades 9 thru 12.
2. SCIENCE: One and one-half (1-1/2) credits—Lab science (1 credit) in 10th-grade Biology.
3. MATHEMATICS: Two and one-half (2-1/2) credits. Must complete successfully the 35 Math objectives.
4. SOCIAL STUDIES: Two and one-half (2-1/2) credits of which one (1) credit will be American History, Grade 11; and one-half (1/2) credit in American Government, Grade 12.
5. ENGLISH LANGUAGE ARTS: Three (3) credits 9 thru 12. To be continually enrolled in English each year. One (1) credit must be earned during the senior year.
6. PHYSICAL EDUCATION: One (1) unit of credit. One-half (1/2) credit is to be taken in both the 9th and 10th grades.
7. Must be enrolled in and complete successfully five (5) credits during the 12th grade.

High School Programs

To provide an educational program widely diversified and differentiated in its course offerings, standards and emphases to serve all youth in one comprehensive high school has been a traditional and long-standing objective of the public high school. Some cities have used separate academic and vocational high schools, but the single high school in which varied programs of study are provided is in general use.

Generally the contemporary secondary school programs emphasize several areas which include general education, specialized training provisions of a wide range and scope, guidance services and special training for handicapped students. The stress on general education including citizenship training and support for liberal training in this country has brought about such a pronounced emphasis on general education that it comprises approximately half of the secondary school offerings. This fundamental program relative to the general education is required

---

*EARLY GRADUATION: To be eligible for early graduation, students must be enrolled in six (6) subjects each year (9-12) and earn 21 credits by the semester of their senior year. Careful attention will be given to past grades, attendance record and good citizenship.

of all high school students. This usually includes a minimum of three or four years of English language, two years of social studies with one year devoted to American history study, one year of mathematics, one year of science and four years devoted to some combination of health and physical education.

Such general education required of all students has been referred to as "required" or "common to all," but the content is not necessarily identical for all students within a school or in all schools. The general education courses are the required courses and the specialized education courses, which are the elective courses, include a sequence of classes that are well defined and provide preparation for advanced study or vocation and personal-interest courses. These offerings comprise practically half the high school offerings. To a great extent the success of the specialized education program is dependent upon the size of a school and the counseling services provided. Such elective courses offered should be determined by the needs and interests of the school. However, in most schools the facilities, staff, resources and number of enrollees determine the course offerings. As students move to a higher grade in secondary schools the time allotted and the specialized course offerings increase noticeably.

Numerous courses are offered in the general education area that motivate students and fulfill needs for future study, careers and vocations. Elective subjects run the gamut from ceramics and sculpture to personal adjustment and marriage. Any student should be able to find courses suited to his needs, interests and abilities, his career or for college prerequisites if he is college-bound. In a typical high school course offerings are in the areas of art, business, industrial arts, foreign language, home economics, vocal and instrumental music, physical education and miscellaneous areas such as teacher aide and library aide.

Student activities outside the regular school day include those concerning personal interests and skills, as well as leadership and talent development. Participation in intramural programs, athletic competition, debate, student government, dramatics, social activities, program planning and various other activities afford students opportunities to relate harmoniously to one another, to cooperate, share, compromise and understand and respect the attitudes, needs and ideas of others as they develop their own personal abilities.

The background information on the public schools that has been given and the additional background material is relevant to an understanding of the role of education in contemporary society and should be a resource for educational reference that all persons, whether in the profession of education or not, should be aware of and should have in their possession. Following the background information on the beginnings, the development and the framework and workings of the schools, the suggestions to meet the challenge of the dilemma the schools are in today will follow. This is a crucial time in education—a time of crisis.

Catholic Schools and Their Educational Implication

A parochial school is maintained as a day school by a religious group. This group is generally coeducational in the lower or elementary grades, but in many instances at the secondary level separate institutions for boys and girls are provided. At the basis of Catholic scholasticism is God, and it is an unchanging basis of action. There underlies the belief that there can be no real purpose of education or aim to living without such a basis.

The history of the Catholic schools as evidenced herein has coincided with the history of education. In parochial schools the curriculum parallels that of the public school except for the religious instruction. Most parochial schools are Roman Catholic. American education must consider Catholic schools when educational implications are involved, for approximately every seventh student in the nation attends a Catholic school. Statistics reveal that since 1940, the number of Catholic parochial elementary and high school students has increased from 2.4 to 5.8 million. Fourteen percent of all American elementary and secondary school students attend Catholic schools. These schools range from kindergartens to medical schools.

Catholic school students are found in many learning institutions throughout the country. They are now found in more than 300 institutions of higher learning and in 2,500 secondary and 10,000 elementary schools. Among the universities are Notre Dame, Georgetown Catholic University of America, St. Louis, Fordham, Boston College, Marquette and St. John's of Brooklyn with an enrollment of 12,000 students. Included also are a number of good smaller schools including St. Peter's in Jersey City, St. Thomas in St. Paul, Minnesota, and Manhattan College in Riverdale, New York.

Some parishes have high school enrollments while others have few students. Some range in tuition fees from a few high-tuition prep schools whose graduates move on to Ivy League colleges to private low-tuition schools or academies directed by Sisters of Mercy, Franciscan friars, Christian Brothers and other teaching orders.

The average tuition some years back ranged from $76 to $100 annually in the parish high schools. The boys' academies and convent schools' tuition was up to $150 and $200 a year. A few of the ultra-private schools, like Park Avenue's Loyola (Jesuit) and the Convents of the

Sacred Heart and Marymount Schools, are exclusively located in such places as Grosse Point, Michigan; Boca Raton, Florida; Upper Fifth Avenue, New York; and Santa Barbara, California.

There are thousands of elementary schools from tiny parish schools to huge suburban classrooms. Today in the inner city the schools' attendance is to an extent by minority groups. Practically all Catholic elementary schools are connected with the parish.

Catholic schools employ some 200,000 teachers, many of whom receive minimal pay and are a part of the church as priests, nuns and brothers. The various sisterhoods of the major convents or the mother-houses receive a part of the very small income their members earn. Such money is used for the care of sick and retired members, the education of young sisters and for the administrative expenses of the order.

The average pay of the lay teachers, which number 65,000, has been less than $4,000 annually, $2,000 below public school standard. Many of these teachers are ill-prepared, underprivileged and always underpaid. They are not as concerned about their low salaries, but their lack of acceptance by their colleagues as professionals bothers them. Among both lay and religious elementary teachers, approximately half have bachelor's degrees. Approximately three-fourths of the Catholic high school teachers are college graduates as compared to the public high schools where practically all teachers have earned degrees.

These Catholic schools are supported by private means and only a few benefit from endowments. Elementary and secondary Catholic schools profit from some federal programs for schools, such as the remedial reading and math programs under Title I. Direct tuition is the means of support for 77 percent of the secondary schools and 50 percent of the elementary. The parishes meet the school costs in some dioceses. A Notre Dame study, which reveals much about the status and operation of Catholic schools, indicates that only thirty-four high schools in the United States receive more than half their income from a bishop's office.

Is education in these schools up with the public school academic standards? How does it compare with public school education? Are those people educated in a monastic setting prepared to adapt in a secular world? Some people are of the opinion that their children will obtain a better education in a parochial school. There seems to be a growing trend of students from public schools and non-Catholics who choose to attend parochial schools. In 1982, 10.6 percent of the 3 million Catholic school students in the country were non-Catholics. In one Kansas City school only 17 percent of the students were Catholic. The most common reasons given for non-Catholic attendance are the discipline and educational programs Catholics provide. Catholic principals say the Catholic school's religious requirements rarely cause problems for the non-Catholic student. Many parents are dissatisfied with their local schools. Another reason for the switch to the Catholic school, according to some parents, is that the public schools have inadequate programs for the gifted.

Some high schools charge a higher tuition for non-Catholics because of the increase of non-Catholics desiring to attend. The Catholics believe those attending are doing so to gain a Christian influence in their education. There are advantages and disadvantages to Catholic schools. On the minus side, teachers have less education, the schools are over-crowded and operate on a smaller budget. On the plus side, Catholic schools can pick and choose their students. Unruly and undisciplined students often end up in public schools. According to comparative re-cords, it is shown that students in Catholic schools are superior in both learning potential and academic achievement. The same Notre Dame study pointed out that the superiority they discovered can be traced largely to the "relatively selective" admissions policies of the schools. Many persons, however, have hurled inferiority charges against these schools.

For the Notre Dame report, thousands of elementary students were administered the Stanford Achievement Test, the Kuhlman-Anderson Test and the Otis Mental Ability Test, the latter two mental ability measures. High school students were given two tests—the Metropolitan Achievement Test, High School Battery, and the Otis Mental Ability Test. The tests concluded that IQs of elementary students averaged 110, a sign to the testers of the superior academic learning potential. Achieve-ment scores at or above the national norms were made by 84 percent. High school students had similar findings. In academic achievement approximately 17 percent exceeded the national norm, and those classi-fied as reaching "total potential" in language arts, social studies, mathe-matics and science reached more than 80 percent.

Other religious groups such as the Lutherans, Christians, Baptists and Adventists operate elementary and secondary schools. These schools emphasize religious training. Although various denominations maintain parochial schools in the United States, most of them are Roman Catholic.

Parish schools in the United States have two meanings. The foregoing ones have been connected with a parochial foundation and maintained by a religious order. The other type of parish school, such as in Louisi-ana, is maintained by the civil parishes or county.

11

Guidance and Counseling

Various services and needs are required by children and youth because of the complexity of individual differences, abilities, interests, background and goals. Students are in need of an authority with professional skills and abilities who has access to records of their abilities, performance and background information to guide them in making proper course choices and helping them adjust to life situations and school. Some students need guidance in learning to get along successfully with classmates and teachers and to aid them in making a success of their total school lives.

To understand this relatively new and highly important field of counseling and guidance, one needs to possess some knowledge of its background and its development as an integral part of the educative process.

To define guidance is not an inconsequential task, rather it is a somewhat difficult one. Authorities disagree on the precise meaning of its terminology. Their definitions vary in breadth from a narrow description, as exemplified by the effort of an adult to help a child realize that prevaricating is misbehavior, to the all-embracing point of view that furthering mental health is the dominant concern of all teaching and must permeate the entire educative process including the guidance program.

According to Dr. Robert Mathewson, in his *Guidance Policy and Practice,* we find ourselves "in a new era of social demand and upon a new level of perspective and practice." He further contends that emphasis upon the social consequences of education and of guidance, requiring a reappraisal of purposes and procedures, characterizes this new period. According to this authority in the field, guidance has a meaning to the parent, to the teacher, to the school administrator, to the national legislator and to the guidance counselor.

To the parent, guidance may mean the general influence exerted in the home while fostering the favorable upbringing of the child, plus whatever special help may be needed in the way of reproof, praise, admonition and advice when difficult situations arise.

Guidance to the teacher may mean simply "good teaching," which entails continuous consideration of individual needs as well as particular attention to individual problems of adjustment or learning when such problems emerge in the setting of the classroom.

To the pupil guidance may be of no essential significance if he fails to come in contact with it in a personal way. If he does, it may involve some form of discipline or a period each week when study habits and one's future are explored.

For the school administrator the concept embodies the foregoing concepts in addition to constituting an indispensable phase of the school program closely allied to instruction and possessing various special service aspects.

An instrument identifying, advising and directing youth is the interpretation of guidance to the national legislator.

Lastly, to the guidance counselor, guidance is conceived as a systematic, continuous, professional process of assisting pupils with definite needs and problems in the areas of school progress, personal-social relations and educational-vocational orientation.

In summation, Mathewson states that "guidance is a process bearing directly upon the adjustment, orientation and development of individual pupils. Guidance activity is something distinct in itself, requiring a policy to direct it, an organized program and set of procedures to fulfill its purposes and professional competence and attitudes to conduct it effectively."

Crow and Crow refer to guidance as "the assistance made available by competent counselors to an individual of any age to help him, direct his own life, develop his own point of view, make his own decisions and carry his own burdens."

A simple but practical and challenging concept of guidance is contained in Hamrin's definition of guidance as "helping John to see through himself in order that he may see himself through."

Another definition which helps to clarify the difference in vocational and personal counseling is that proposed by Super, who points out that the modern emphasis in vocational counseling involves a process of helping the individual in three ways: "to develop and accept an integrated and adequate picture of self; to relate this concept of self to the environmental world; and to establish goals and develop plans in accordance with this self-environment configuration."

Endless definitions of guidance as seen in the perspective of endless authorities could be given, but the basic thesis is similar in each—that of helping the individual understand himself in self situations, to make adjustments to his self-situational field in a manner which will enable him to gain self-satisfaction and to develop his potentialities in order to reach goals attainable by him.

Following will be a review of the evolutionary processes of guidance from its inception to the present and the philosophical bases involved in its progression and implementation. Although the idea of counseling is as old as man himself, for the usage here its development will begin with a brief look into early ideas of helping people with emphasis on the end of the nineteenth century forward to guidance as we know it today.

Development of the Guidance Movement

Interest in human welfare and adjustment is not new or of recent origin. Down through the ages, among all types and conditions of people there have been attempts made at helping individuals to discover their potentialities, to analyze their personalities or to predict their future life experiences. Many of these guidance practices were crude and based upon superstitions, while others developed into elaborate and intricate systems of analysis predictions.

Nonscientific "predicting" includes various fields and thoughts, such as: numerology, graphology, astrology, palmistry, physiognomy, phrenology, occultism, spiritualism, dream interpretation, "fortune-telling" by the use of tea leaves, coffee grounds and playing cards and the application of various kinds of superstition associated with the traditions of a people. Even in our modern twentieth century, some of these techniques still wield considerable influence upon the behavior of many youth and adults as well.

The nonscientific approach of numerology or the attitudes toward numbers is based upon the premise that man is surrounded by numerous vibrations, each of which emanates from a particular number. Scientific data to this time, however, has disproved the validity of numerology. Patterning one's life course to this technique is ineffectual, if not dangerous.

Coming down from ancient time is another pseudoscientific cult—that of associating one's fate with the stars or astrology. Although scientific research in this area has not substantiated claims made by astrologists, many people continue to believe in the efficacy of this method of "guidance."

Graphology, another pseudoscientific technique, is the analysis of character in terms of an individual's penmanship pattern. Except in definitely pronounced deviations from the accepted norms of penmanship, there is very minor validity to be of significance in handwriting as a measure of one's personality.

The belief that one's hand determines his destiny may be traced back to olden times, particularly in Greece, where it was thought that the kind of person one was held a close alliance to the form and shape of his hand. As a matter of scientific principle, palmistry has failed to qualify for the claims made for it by its proponents.

More closely allied to modern interpretation of personality is phrenology or the technique of character analysis. It is based upon the interpretation of brain action as explained by the faculty psychologists of the nineteenth century; specific forms of mental activity are localized in specific brain areas. This interpretation of brain action, like the foregoing pseudoscientific principles, has been discounted. It has been proved that there is little if any relationship between the size and shape of the average person's head with his degree of possession of one or another specific trait.

The probability of physiognomy that experiences or inner attitudes may have upon facial characteristics also has been discredited. Other predicting techniques have been found to be inconsequential as determinants of personality and behavior. Among these are dreams, occultism and spiritualism.

As early as 1895, a systematic vocational guidance program was developed at the California School of Mechanical Arts in San Francisco. This program provided an experience of an exploratory nature in each of the trades offered in the school, analysis of the individual, counseling, job placement and follow-up procedures on former students.

The most monumental impetus to counseling, however, seems to have been given by Frank Parsons's organization in 1908 of the Vocational Bureau, which was devoted fundamentally to assisting young people to make vocational choices based upon their occupational aptitudes and interests. Parsons also introduced the term "vocational guidance," which he described as a process designed to aid young students in choosing an occupation, in preparing themselves for it, in finding an opening in it and in building up an efficient and successful career. Parsons's original definition is essentially the same as that currently accepted by the National Vocational Guidance Association, which maintains that "Vocational Guidance is the process of assisting the individual to choose an occupation, prepare for it, enter upon it and progress in it."

Since Parsons considered counseling to be essentially a guidance service, shortly after the Vocational Bureau was established he announced a plan for training counselors whose purpose was to prepare young men to become vocational counselors and to manage vocational bureaus in connection with YMCAs, schools, colleges, universities, public school systems, associations and business establishments throughout the country. In 1909, through the efforts of the Vocational Bureau of Boston, one counselor-teacher was appointed for each elementary school and high school in Boston. These teachers were not released from their teaching duties, however, and lacked the necessary tools, supplies and materials for the implementation of their duties.

In 1910, Louis P. Nash was designated to investigate and recommend plans for the establishment of vocational guidance in the Boston schools. By means of lectures by experts, books and visits to business and professional establishments, he suggested that a number of typical occupations be carefully studied.

The following year, Frank P. Goodwin organized a guidance program in the Cincinnati, Ohio, schools. Between 1909 and 1913, Richard D. Allen, while affiliated with the Boston Vocational Bureau, produced many pamphlets and books concerned with vocational opportunities and requirements and initiated conferences with the Boston school counselors. Because of the groundwork laid by both Nash and Allen, the Vocational Information Department was established in Boston in 1913.

In 1915, the Department of Vocational Guidance was organized in Boston. Approximately twelve programs of guidance were established during the first ten years following the establishment of the Vocational Bureau of Boston.

Other national developments included the founding in 1933 of the National Occupational Conference (NOC) and its establishment in 1936 of the Occupation Index, which issued periodically an annotated index of books and pamphlets relating to the broad field of guidance services. The growth of a number of major professional organizations and the publication of several important books—*Aptitudes and Aptitude Testing* by Bingham and *Job Satisfaction* by Robert Hoppock—gave increased momentum to the guidance movement.

Impetus was also given when a national committee of educators in 1938 recommended an expanded program for vocational education. In October, 1938, the U.S. Office of Education established the Occupation and Information Service; funds for this service were authorized by the George-Deen Act. Further progress for guidance activities has come about in the way of governmental support through the passage in 1958 of the National Defense Education Act, administered by the U.S. Office of Education. Two titles in this act have a direct bearing on the functioning of guidance: Title IV, National Defense Fellowships; Title V, Guidance, Counseling and Testing: Identification and Encouragement of Able Students. Research projects and other programs under the National Defense Act have stimulated the growth of the guidance movement in America.

The evolution of guidance services has not been an isolated movement. A change in our culture to one of increased social complexity has placed the responsibility for the practical guidance of young people and the development of value structures on the schools. Concurrently have come developments in the behavioral sciences which have affected the concepts of the purpose and organization of school guidance programs. Guidance services at this time are expected to take the initiative in making the school actively concerned for the student's mental health and social and emotional life as well as for his academic and vocational achievement; in short, guidance work is often referred to as "pupil personnel services" and involves the responsibility for the child's total school experience and, to a degree, for his interdependent home and community experience.

Modern guidance services, building upon new developments in the behavioral sciences, now seek to provide a rich variety of aids to children and youth to enable them to make use of all that is known about environment and growth in discovering for themselves satisfying roles in our complex society.

Philosophical Bases for the Implementation of Guidance

According to Wrenn in Nelson B. Henry's *Personnel Services in Education,* personnel service in education involves several underlying principles:

>   1. It is predicated upon seeing the learner totally. One must attempt to see him beyond the classroom as a person with a life which is more heavily nonschool than school oriented.
>   2. The student must be treated with dignity; his integrity and right to self-fulfillment must be respected.
>   3. Personnel work must be concerned with the student's plans for the future, as well as concerning itself with his present life.
>   4. Personnel workers must be the prime advocates of the individual differences—respecters of uniqueness.
>   5. Upon its implementation depends a varied methodology—one fitted to the ends to be served. The means of meeting both personal and group experiences should be appropriate to the ends and subordinate to them.
>   6. The quality of the relationship between worker and learner, worker and colleague is the important element in all personnel services.
>   7. Personnel service must remain in the central area of educational effort.

Research upon which the field of guidance is designed is largely borrowed and is behavior research from developmental, educational or clinical psychology, group research from sociology or group dynamics and administrative models from business.

Philosophy and psychology may be thought of as being complimentary because while one contributes to the understanding of truth, the other contributes to an understanding of human behavior within the broader sphere of total existence. Psychology may be defined as a science, a systematic ordering of observations of human behavior. The meaning of this behavior within the cosmos, the nature of the knowledge possessed, the nature of behavior and of existence itself is the province of philosophy. Various philosophies depend upon empiric observations or practical experiences, and their logic and reality is the logic and reality of science. Philosophy antedated all sciences as we now know them.

To gain a true perspective of the involvements of counseling, one must consider some dimensions of philosophy. Several theories to be briefly considered are theories of reality, nature of knowledge, values and relation of ideas. The theory of reality or metaphysics deals with the nature of existence itself, of the nature of the origin of the universe, of man, his purpose, his free will and of the nature of God. The meaning and purpose of human behavior seeks its meaning and purpose through philosophy and religion.

The second theory, the nature of knowledge, which is called epistemology, deals with the possibility of knowing reality, with the importance of and instruments or ways of knowledge. This is of importance in education with the empiricist's approach through observation and the experience of the senses in direct antithesis to the rationalist's dependence upon reason as the source of knowledge.

The third theory, that of values (axiology), is concerned with the nature and kinds of values. In any philosophical system involving education, grave consideration is placed upon values.

The theory of the relation of ideas or logic is closely related to epistemology. Often called the science of reasoning, it is concerned with methods of thinking.

The selection of systems of philosophy most important and significant to student personnel work is complex, for this work is an integral part of the total education program, not separate from other segments of instructional activity; therefore, it is concerned with philosophies of most significance to formal education as a whole. It is most directly concerned with the voluntary aspect of the educational experience and deals with matters concerning self-involvement, which calls for self-understanding and personal planning. This work deals with social living and human interaction. Kinds of learning contributed to are self-learning, social-interaction learning and values of learning.

Among the most systematic of these philosophies is Rationalism (Neo-Humanism, Rational Humanism). One of the oldest of Western world philosophies, with its principal author, Aristotle, it asserts that the essence of human nature is rational character. Man, endowed with reason, is to use this reason in order to know the world in which he lives. Its principal characteristics include the fact that the essence of reality is a system of rational principles, everywhere the same, defining the nature of and man's place in the universe and the cultivation of reason as education's chief aim. Expounded by Adler, Hutchins and Mark Van Doren, the rationalists of today believe that truths exist in the writings of classical thinkers and that man must discover and apply them to current situations.

A second philosophy is Idealism. Idealism is the conclusion that the universe is an expression of intelligence and will, that the enduring substance of the world is of the nature of mind, that the material is explained by the mental. This theory predicates that ideas are absolute—eternal—and this aspect makes it akin to Rationalism.

Realism, a third philosophy, is a scientific product of the twentieth century. Ultimate reality to the realist lies in objects and situations external to the human mind in the "real" or objective world. The realist believes that objects may exist apart from the knowledge process, that acts are disclosed by acts of cognition. Realism, then, is objective, makes use of scientific findings, sees empiric truth as approximating but not necessarily equaling reality.

The fourth and most modern philosophy, Experimentalism (Pragmatism or Instrumentalism), American in its development and emphasis, has as its developers William James and John Dewey. This theory devotes its attention to a theory of knowledge and a theory of values and has had a forceful impact upon education. Its key word is "continuity." The proponents of this philosophy are concerned with phenomena, with a phenomenon. The context of knowing is fixed by a single problem or set of problems, and its most fruitful assumptions emphasize integration, not separation of problem and solution.

Experimentalism is not rationalistic; it does not begin with universal truths but with specific and particular experience. The present and future are stressed. Here values have no existence in themselves but are results of human choices involving a person and his environment.

Existentialism, the last philosophy to be examined, had as its early developers Kierkegaard, Nietzche and Dostoyevsky and is a product of nineteenth-century Europe. Existentialism is concerned with human longing—with man as seeking and needing importance in himself. It believes that experimentalism lacks sufficient concepts of the wholeness of man, that it is based upon the advent of an ideal man. This philosophy may be religious or nonreligious. It assumes that man is important and irreplaceable.

It seems highly probable and practically feasible that the student personnel worker, at times, may feel a need to inculcate and use any one or parts of these philosophies. He must not rely on philosophy alone, but must be affected greatly by psychology as well, for psychology contributes far more than philosophy in that it seeks the reality of human behavior, not human nature. It must be conclusive, then, that the student must draw elements from various existing theories of behavior if he is to fully develop a personality understanding that encompasses the existing needs of his task.

The future of guidance practices, therefore, lies in an approaching convergence of two streams of understanding—both philosophy and psychology. The goals of education must be realistic in terms of what man can do and what he is. More recent guidance efforts today are based upon study and research in the natural and social sciences. There has developed an increased understanding of the psychology of human behavior and of the significance of environmental conditions in the life of an individual. The future in guidance is bright in that the purposes of guidance may be carried to fruition as it seeks to improve the ability of the individual to understand self and environment and to deal with self-situational relations for greater personal satisfaction and social usefulness in the light of social and moral values.

A Philosophy of the Guidance Program

During the last quarter of a century, there have been few movements in American education that have progressed so steadily as guidance. School attendance has come to include practically all youth whether public, private or church-oriented, so it has become increasingly apparent that learning resources in group situations have held little or no meaning for many students. Because of the insufficiency of meaningful experiences and personal contact, the need for guidance has developed. Some students are shackled by intellectual limitations, some by discipline inadequacies, some by lack of self-confidence and self-assurance. Schools and education must be the instruments to dismantle these limitations, to enable students to be free to learn, to not be inhibited and to encourage them to advance not just as others do, but to their own potentialities.

It became apparent early in the century that these many disciplines had developed techniques, processes and materials that needed to be incorporated and made available to aid the development of the individual. Guidance, a new discipline, embodying its own philosophy, came into being and began to become organized. Thus, as an organized discipline guidance belongs to the century even though most of its techniques and theories were developed earlier by other disciplines, such as psychology, education, philosophy, sociology and the like.

A philosophy must be the basis for the establishment of an organization for a guidance program. The development of guidance hypotheses and action guidelines determines the organizational structure. Special techniques and materials are used in implementing the guidance program. Maximum benefits are achieved by all individuals involved when these fundamentals are unified ideally into a viable and working arrangement.

The rapidity with which guidance has developed in American schools has been brought about by new social and technological conditions and needs, by the emphasis of individual differences and by the evolving of a self-concept by each individual, by a new technique for studying individuals and by the enlarged concept of viewing the school as a social institution.

The underlying basic philosophy of guidance has as its tenet that of helping each student achieve his maximum personal development. Guidance is viewed as a developmental process, one which is essentially concerned with helping students assess their needs, develop their potentialities, accept and use these abilities, develop their life's goals and formulate plans of action in making these purposes become actualities.

Guidance is twofold; it is a concept and a process. As a concept, it is an idea, a generalization of what should be the optimal development of the individual for his and society's benefit. As a process, guidance is the operation or act of acquiring and collecting information of the developing characteristics and patterns of the student and assisting him in using this knowledge for his personal growth and achievement. Every factor which influences the welfare of the student must be considered and acted upon in his best interest if needed in directing his maximal development in school.

The Guidance Counselor

The guidance services in schools today have become an integral and important part of the educational program at all levels. Most persons in the field of education agree on the importance of and necessity for its inclusion in the school's programs, because through guidance the counselor works toward helping individuals to know their abilities, their strengths and weaknesses, to develop them to their fullest extent, to relate them to their life's vocational choices and goals and to help them mature in self-guidance and in the ability to solve their own problems.

A trained guidance counselor should have certain qualifications, including being an individual who is well adjusted and is highly knowledgeable of the purpose and extent of the guidance program and its relationship to the school's total program. The counselor must be able to work effectively with students, teachers, administrative personnel and parents; the counselor should be one who has the respect and confidence of all students and who practices confidentiality unless the problem could bring discomfort or harm to the student. The counselor must meet the minimum standards for certification and must be able to recognize the necessity for securing information important to counseling needs. The extent to which the students, teachers, administrators and community use the resources of the guidance services determines its effectiveness.

The guidance counselor maintains a cumulative record file of each student from the beginning of his schooling. This cumulative record contains personal data, home and family record, course outline and class record, grades, test scores, health information, promotion record and other items relative to gaining an overall picture of his student's progress.

Counselors aid students when problems arise with other students and teachers. When students face difficulty in schoolwork, the counselor aids them in working through these problems, which interfere with their learning. The counselor provides referral services if they are needed within the school or through community agencies and guides the student in his class enrollments and in making class changes when needed. Through conferences with students, teachers and often the parents, counselors understand better how the student feels about himself, school, classmates and his home environment, thus the counselor is able to suggest helps for parents and teachers and aids the student in realizing what is needed for him to improve himself and to adjust satisfactorily to both his school and home setting.

While older students have problems such as concerns on sex, dating, drugs, pregnancy and the like, young children have problems adjusting to school, home and getting along with classmates. Through individual and group counseling, a counselor is trained to help students discuss the problems more freely. Should problems arise that are too deep-seated for the counselor to handle, a referral is made to the proper agency. If the referral is to a community agency, the parents usually must be involved.

The counselor also consults with parents, teachers and school personnel in helping students adjust and solve various problems. Because of the counselor's special training, suggestions, alternatives and techniques for the student's adjustment are given. Often counselors may make referrals to the school nurse if the student is experiencing vision, hearing or other health problems which may be corrected or improved through special services of school specialists or referrals to area health agencies. Referrals may be made to the school social worker if the problem involves a home situation or a school problem requiring the social worker's skills.

Peer pressure, boy-girl relationships, sexual awakening, parent relationships, acceptance problems, classwork and teacher problems confront middle school and junior high students. The adolescent needs a confidante to whom he may go to talk with, someone who will be straightforward with him and will help him. The student gains support and confidence in himself when he has someone who has an objective, but not a judgmental ear. Students are led to see that their problems are not different from those that other adolescents experience. Through careful guidance, the counselor gives information on dating, personal appearance, sex, birth control, pregnancy, venereal disease, alcohol, drugs and cigarettes.

Through group discussions, or individual sessions, counselors may help students share ideas on attitudes and behavior changes, parental relationships and may provide an avenue for open discussion on information which previously had been inhibited.

As early as elementary school, the counselor may begin giving students an opportunity to think about and look into a future career. Although students' ideas as to their life's vocation may change many times, introduction to careers should be started early.

The primary role of the counselor in light of the foregoing information is that of individual counseling. The counselor is expected to provide professional leadership for all of the guidance services, information and the use of other techniques to insure the maximum adjustment of every student.

Only if a guidance program has the enthusiastic endorsement of the administrator will it be effective. He is the school's executive officer and is responsible for the administrative functions of the guidance program. Assistance may be given the counselor in its program development by a carefully chosen guidance committee and in-service faculty training through teachers' meetings and workshops. Although the number of students a full-time counselor serves varies, the maximum number has been considered to be 300 to 500, and at least 50 percent of the counselor's time should be devoted to individual conferences with the remaining time for performing other duties relevant to counseling. However, in many schools only approximations of the above numbers and percentages can be adhered to.

Testing

One of the important duties of the counselor is to give various types of tests and interpret their meaning to students, parents and teachers; such a function requires specialized training. All tests except achievement tests, which are used for instructional purposes, should be given by the counselor. Test results enable the counselor, the teacher and parents to understand the strengths and weakneses of the students. This enables the student to exercise more effort in areas of difficulty, to know what courses to take and what direction to pursue in a vocation or college-bound program. Tests also serve as a measure of comparison with local and national test scores. Intelligence tests which yield IQs serve as an indicator of the ability of students and often are the determinants to a degree, in the class program a student is in and the courses he may take.

Tests such as achievement tests serve to ascertain what students have learned up to the testing time. A good counselor, however, realizes that many influences affect resulting test scores and involve physical fitness at testing time, testing environment, reading ability and the background of the student.

Special testing of students having learning difficulties, severe behavioral problems, or advanced levels of learning are given individualized testing by a school psychologist to ascertain whether there exists a need for special placement as for slow learners, learning disabled or gifted or the need for special services, like a speech or a hearing therapist. Such definitive testing for these special cases are the province of the school psychologist.

In one school district scores on Stanford Achievement Tests, in addition to academic performance and age and grade level requirements, determine the acceptance of students to a learning center for the academically accelerated students. The Sumner Academy of Arts and Sciences in Kansas City, Kansas, Public School District 500, was opened in August, 1978.

The court-ordered desegregation plan of the federal government brought about the closing of two all-black schools, Northeast Junior High School and Sumner High School, both with all black students and integrated faculties; this action proved to be the catalyst that brought about the accelerated learning center. It was ruled that there was no such thing as separate but equal schools. Other desegregation had been started in Kansas City, Kansas, in the late 1950s. The Sumner Academy is designed to meet the particular needs, interests and challenges of those students in grades 8–12 who are academically talented and intellectually oriented. This type of educational institution was new to Kansas City. Qualified, experienced instructors teach a highly structured and keenly enriched curriculum in language arts, math, science and foreign languages. The courses are geared toward meeting college requirements. Opportunities for classes in elective courses such as business, music, home economics and others are available.

Services for College-Bound Students

Students planning to attend college need the counselor's assistance in being certain to enroll in the proper courses for college-bound students. Other pertinent information should be made available such as college entrance examinations, national scholarship examinations and information on local scholarships. Directories and guides to various colleges and universities should be available to students. These guides and information bulletins contain entrance requirements, information concerning the school, fees, course offerings and supportive services being offered including financial aid. College fairs are held in many high schools each year with college representatives present to inform students of the college's offerings and for recruitment. Counselors should be able to make suggestions on colleges that would be suitable for a student taking into consideration the student's academic performance, test scores and career interests.

Placement Services in Guidance

A comprehensive guidance program includes three types of placement services. These include educational, occupational or job and social. Such services aid students while in school, upon leaving school and upon entering a career later in life. To identify opportunities or alternatives having the greatest potential for aiding in the development of students is a purpose of placement services. It may aid students in fulfilling course requirements or may help financially.

For a student to gain from the placement services, it is necessary that he is involved in counseling guidance services. Included are services of testing, measurement and individual appraisal. Articulation from one school to another is important in continuing the continuity of the educational process. This transition should be smooth, uncomplicated and provide experiences which will enable the student to adjust quickly and satisfactorily. Counselors and administrators have worked to ease the strain of change such as inviting the incoming students to an orientation program before school begins, visitation days for students and their parents and invitations to various activities. Placement at different grade levels warrants attention as students choose courses that should be beneficial and courses which add to their educational growth. Should work-study services be available in the higher grades, students should be alerted to this program early in their school life.

An understanding of the strengths and weaknesses of a student aids the counselor in helping the student make realistic vocational choices— choices in which he is capable of succeeding. As a result of encouragement to gain work experience in part-time employment, students are in a position to understand the aspects of work, what one is expected to do, to learn to be responsible, punctual, dependable and to promote acceptable interaction with others as he, at the same time, gains satisfaction in being productive and in performing a good job.

Follow-up Services

Follow-up services are important to the evaluation of the counselor services in ascertaining the extent of services given an individual or groups of individuals. Various surveys of some type should be ongoing, for they are important in revealing progress made by graduates and dropouts. Follow-up is time consuming, so there is usually no consistency in its operation. Most follow-up, or follow-through as it is sometimes referred to, is made at the high school level, but elementary and upper grades benefit also. Several methods for follow-up services may be used, such as a short, well-worded questionnaire, personal interviews with individuals or groups and letters or telephone calls to former students.

The results of the follow-through survey considering their subjectivity will provide information that will be helpful in modifying or improving counselor services. Some type of research or survey in use often improves guidance services, promotes understanding of the guidance program and develops among the school staff an interest and favorable attitude toward such research projects and findings and stimulates school and community interests. Research activities will be dealt with more fully in the following section.

Research Activities in the Guidance Program

The research service of the guidance program should be a continuous process which is carried out through projects conducted as a part of the total guidance program. The statistical data from these research projects are beneficial for several reasons. They aid in increasing the effectiveness of the guidance program, supplying information for evaluation, producing innovative ideas, providing revealing facts and stimulating the additional uses of such research results.

The assistance of the school personnel is important in any type of research project because they will compile data, analyze information and determine its usefulness to the guidance staff. Research is an important part of the guidance program, and its end result should be new ideas, implications, relationships and developments. Anyone responsible for the research service must be fully aware of its purposes, for they will lend assistance in designing, identifying and carrying out research projects. Six fundamental purposes of this research service are: (1) to improve the effectiveness of the guidance program, (2) to supply information relative to the guidance program, (3) to sort and collate all available information, thereby producing new data which is applicable to the total population served by the guidance program and to various groups in that population, (4) to promote local research, (5) to promote a favorable attitude among the staff toward research projects and findings and (6) to stimulate interest in the importance of research and in the use of the research findings.

The responsibility for reporting and interpreting these findings for the benefit of the guidance counselor, faculty, administrators, students, parents and other community persons will be the duty of the person responsible for the research service.

In performing such a research project four major items must be considered. They include the purpose, method, technique and area being studied. Although each item is distinct in itself, they are all related. Four basic methods of approach are important in performing research. They are the historical method, normative survey or descriptive method, experimental method and the prognostic or predictive method.

The Historical Method

When records and reports have been prepared, the historical method is used. A review is made and the information gained is sorted and collated into a form that would have additional meaning for the present program. This particular research is used to identify trends, various types of services and techniques, as well as activities and successes of programs offered in the past. This method is a retrospective view of the past.

The Normative Survey or Descriptive Method

The present practice in the guidance program is the focus of the collection of data in this method of research. This method has merit in the gathering of information pertinent to knowledge, opinions and attitudes of the nature and quality of the guidance program. This method serves as a source of obtaining information for evaluation service. The normative survey determines what is now taking place.

Experimental Method

This method is a scientific approach wherein a project design is outlined as a control of known variables under experimental conditions. In this method it is possible to make a statement of probability when there is participation by one group in guidance services and nonparticipation by another. This is done at the completion of a project. Gathering data for comparative evaluation of differing approaches or for statistical tests of hypotheses is a use for this method.

Prognostic or Predictive Method

This method is used in showing the relationship between two or more factors by the use of statistical correlations or prediction tables. This predictive method could be used in forecasting or predicting an academic grade according to percentile rank on a definite standardized test. This predictive method determines probable occurrences under certain conditions.

Having research consultants is somewhat in the experimental stage today and very few schools employ them. The guidance counselor serves in this capacity in many schools; however, the consultants are increasing in number. Each person involved in research must know what his responsibilities are if a research service is to be effective.

Research Projects

Projects engaged in by a school will change yearly. Various projects will receive special attention while others may receive only enough notice to complete the project. Constant attention must be given to the timing of the project. Many different research projects may be undertaken by a school. Some of the most common follow:

1. Reduction of scholastic failures due to the influence of counseling service.
2. Effect of a definite guidance activity on the rate of dropouts.
3. Correlation of academic marks and scholastic abilities within a department, a building or in specific courses.
4. Relation of school curriculum to career employment.
5. The validity of tests developed through correlation of test data with uses made locally of the test data.

6. Group guidance and its relation to modification of individual expectation.

7. Changes in counselor image due to the modification of guidance service.

8. Participation of faculty in the guidance program.

9. Development of local norms on standardized tests.

10. Extent of guidance information supplied by faculty.

11. Types of guidance needed in elementary schools or other school levels.

12. Recognition of change in specific groups of students at stages throughout their school years.

Approval to engage in these research projects must be received from he proper personnel before they are begun. Careful consideration hould be given to having the proper facilities, competent personnel and dequate materials and equipment when such research is undertaken. 'he type of materials necessary for a project under consideration will epend upon the needs of the project. Special materials are not needed or all research. As the research service expands, so will reference naterials and books. When standardized tests are used, test-scoring alculators and machines are needed. Larger projects require data pro-essing equipment. A budget should include any research project con-emplated. It is important that periodic evaluation be made of research ervices.

12

Public Relations in Guidance

We must strive continually to implement and support those areas of the educational field which will provide satisfactory working relations with the people whom we serve, the people with whom we work and the students who come under our tutelage in our American system of education.

Public relations is a comparatively new field in the administration of schools with possibilities for growth that have been explored little. The importance of public relations in the field of education was not formally recognized until recently and provision made for it in the management of educational institutions.

Man, in order to fulfill his individual and group needs, has created an array of social institutions. Those institutions, which are maintained as a means to an end and which the people can modify or eliminate at will, are democratic social institutions. The people exercise a high degree of control over public education through their partnership with government, through their retention of the right to differ and through the planning of educational activities in the organization of their schools.

The effective functioning of democratic institutions is dependent upon how well the public is kept aware of the purpose, the value and the conditions and needs of their institutions. If education is as important as we believe, we are obligated to learn how to use all honest means of leading people to understand and support it adequately. Neglect to do so is an evasion of ethical and professional responsibility. At this time, when education is of unprecedented importance to individuals and to the nation, honest and effective public communication designed to create the greatest amount of awareness and understanding is a responsibility of education leaders. In a society of free, responsible citizens, people have a right to information and ideas which will enable them to make intelligent educational choices and decisions.

Public Relations Defined

Public relations or the planned effort to influence opinion through acceptable performance and two-way communications in a broad sense bears the same principles of school public relations in which these relations are seen as a process of communication between the school and the community for the purpose of increasing citizen understanding of educational needs and practices and encouraging intelligent citizen interest and cooperation in improving the schools. Public relations in the guidance program is important. Although guidance is a relatively new service, one which has not always been considered essential, its impact is far-reaching. A good guidance program, therefore, will provide the need for such a program and establish the methods to be used.

Public Relations in Guidance

Hollis and Hollis, in *Organizing for Effective Guidance,* define public relations in guidance as "the organized effort of guidance personnel to obtain information about the existing guidance program, its philosophy and its needs and dissemination to administrators, faculty, parents, students and others in the community."

By means of public relations, information is disseminated concerning the guidance program, its philosophy, existing services and further needs. The scope of public relations encompasses obtaining and setting forth information; aiding in the understanding and interpretation of this information in relation to individuals, their needs, problems and environment and fostering goodwill.

The counselor must be a public relations specialist in order to stimulate and sell the guidance program. We may ask: What are some of the implications involved in selling a guidance program? What is to be done? To whom and where should we turn? Following are suggested methods of fostering good and effective public relations regarding the guidance program.

Objectives in Guidance

The interpretive methods of school public relations are those of teaching or of education. They operate best when they are kept in the open. The purpose of public relations in counseling is a social operation. Change can be anticipated through the formation of public opinion, which is predicated upon free and open discussion terminating in conviction.

The purposes for public relations must be established in relation to situations locally. The purposes include:

• Collecting and dispersing information concerning the guidance program.
• Introducing and acquainting people with the program.
• Providing detailed and comprehensive overview of the guidance program.
• Promoting clearer understanding and interpretation of facts.
• Creating a readiness for the modification of existing services or the introduction of a new service or activity.
• Initiating and stimulating participation, cooperation and enthusiasm by others.
• Providing such an effective and workable program that its success is contingent upon the intelligent, active and continuous participation of everyone involved.

Developing Guidelines in Public Relations Programs

Certain guidelines should be adhered to in the development of public relations programs. Although the actual responsibility for public relations relating to guidance is upon the guidance staff members, each guidance worker must be cognizant of the fact that the school has a schoolwide public relations program that will be supplemented by the work of the guidance staff.

The first guideline is that guidance should be an integral and working part of the total school program. To do this several rules must be realized and followed. All public relations releases or memos and all guidance activities should be approved by the proper authorities. This would include the principal, the assistant principal if he has anything to do with the guidance program and the director of guidance or the superintendent if the principal feels their consent is needed. Public relations must be a continuous and ongoing process. Public relations should be made an organized effort with long-range planning and emphasis on the total school program for which the guidance services function. These services and the individuals responsible for carrying them out must remain in harmony with the policies of the school and discuss differences, should they arise, with the proper authorities rather than with the public.

Another guideline to be remembered is that in developing public relations programs it is well to remember that public relations is the assembling and dispersing of information that is helpful to the students and to the community. Work should be directed toward the inclusion of people into the active and continuous participation in the guidance program; interest and enthusiasm must be kept alive. Helpful information on social programs, jobs and the like must be gathered and dispersed to build a better program that will be of benefit to the youth of the community. Keep the program viable and build on the present foundation. Recognize what has been done in the school and plan future work with those actively engaged in carrying out the program. Keep a balanced emphasis on the various programs.

The third guideline deals with public relations releases. All releases for various groups should be written from the viewpoint of the receiver and in simple and understandable language for the people for whom it is intended.

The public should know something of the policies and principles of guidance and also the areas in which the guidance staff is expected to offer and direct its services. Recipients should be involved in the program to the extent that they will want to participate.

Another guideline is that in carrying out the public relations activities all available media are needed with the approval of the proper authorities by involving various community groups.

The last guideline points up that with the many activities involved the responsibility for coordinating the program should be delegated to one qualified individual. The individual should have a sincere interest in public relations, the ability to express himself concisely, clearly and intelligibly. The person should also possess a thorough understanding of the field of guidance. A definite time for guidance activities particularly directed toward public relations activities should be included within the guidance schedule.

The coordinator of the public relations program is not the only person directly concerned with the program. In addition, the other members of the guidance staff should aid not only in planning the public relations program, but also in its implementation. Everyone associated in the school in the field of guidance has an important role in public relations. Should the school have a guidance committee, it, too, functions with the counselors.

As the guidance staff works with individuals much information should be gained that is of importance to each other. New insights not imagined before may be gained, and the guidance staff may be able to use information in many helpful ways when it has been assimilated and surveyed. Each member of the guidance department should be in a better position to disseminate some of the same kinds of information, thus keeping both the students and the community well informed with comprehensive, uniform and pertinent information helpful to all concerned.

The Teacher and Public Relations in Guidance

Undoubtedly the teacher is the most important cog in the public relations wheel. The teacher's day-to-day relations with the students determine to a great extent the way in which the parents regard the school. The teacher determines the success of the school and the instructional effectiveness of that teacher is the most vital force in the creation of public opinion—good or bad—concerning the school.

Just as the teacher's role in the public relations of the school is important, it also is important to the guidance program. Good teaching is the teacher's major contribution to school public relations. However, the teacher may add to his effectiveness by supplementing the classroom expertise of his school public relations activity with various social relationships.

Teachers must realize that they must take an active part in the development of the guidance program. It is through the teachers that students gain their information on guidance.

Teachers must be consulted, listened to, kept aware of what is being done and helped as much as possible to maintain good relationships with students, parents and the community. Many teachers feel counselors at times are not helpful, but they must realize what they think is the answer is not always the workable one for the child's best interests. The teacher who finds a counselor understanding, patient, cooperative and willing to lend assistance in understanding a child and his problems is more likely to accept the counselor and his assistance. The teacher, first of all, must accept the organized guidance program which will help him become more effectively involved in the program.

With the principal's permission and suggestions the following ideas may be used to inform the teachers of the guidance program, thus furthering good public relations between the teacher and the counselor:

- Welcome faculty members new to the building and aid them in meeting other staff members and in making adjustments.
- Early in the school year plan an orientation program with the administration and staff to acquaint the teachers with the guidance program.
- Teachers may be given a handbook which contains a thorough explanation of the guidance services.

- In-service training sessions are helpful to the teachers. Study aspects of the guidance program may be discussed.
- Solicit the help of teachers in giving tests. They may provide students with a pencil when needed or just be around to lend comfort to the students when they see a familiar face.
- Brief bulletins may be issued periodically to keep faculty abreast of guidance activities and other pertinent information.
- Assist teachers with professional and personal problems where needed or if advice is sought.
- Selected current guidance activities—local, statewide and national— may be placed in counselors' offices, the library and the teachers' lounge that they may be easily accessible to the teachers.
- Let teachers become aware of the part they play in the guidance program—making referrals, homeroom guidance programs, records to be kept concerning students and the reading of bulletins.
- Aid teachers in arranging parent-teacher conferences.
- Be mindful of teacher requests in making schedule changes or in arranging schedules to aid in student adjustment.
- Commend or recognize in some manner faculty members and others who have been of help in serving the needs of students or of groups when such recognition is warranted.

To foster better public relations with teachers the following concerns are helpful:

- Be friendly and cordial with the teachers.
- The names of all teachers in the building should be learned early. Call them by name.
- Enable teachers to have some free time when talking with students and when enrolling students in their classes if the teachers' help is not needed.
- Counselors should be friendly with the administration, but they are not one of them. Teachers must be aware of this.
- Additional duties should be given sparingly to teachers. For the most part, they are usually overburdened.
- The subject matter and methods of a teacher should not be criticized. Be diplomatic if changes are needed.
- When tests results are returned, make the results available to teachers and students with explanations of their meanings.

The teacher who is effective realizes that his job is one of importance and he expects others to think so, too. The effective teacher possesses special skills, knowledge and expertise in performing his job. These abilities are of value in the implementation of a workable guidance program.

The Student and Public Relations

The students in a school can be the most active participants in the public relations program; however, they are often the most overlooked. Administrators and teachers take them for granted and fail to realize that students are eager to act as ambassadors of goodwill for their schools.

The important role which the student plays in the daily operation of the school places him automatically in a public relations role in which he interprets the school as it appears to him, to his classmates, his parents and other members of the community.

Many students are not aware of the counselor's role in the school. Oftentimes when they are called to the counselor's office, they feel they are in trouble; however, they generally have a positive attitude toward the program. It is important to begin early to make the student cognizant of what the school has to offer and how the counselor can help the student in the school environment. Just as for teachers. so it is advisable to have some type of orientation for students at the beginning of the year. Several procedures may be used. The orientation may be an orientation assembly, may be printed in the school handbook or may be in the homeroom or teacher advisory groups. Regardless of the method to be used, opportunity for feedback must be given. By careful observation of each year's presentation, it is possible to provide continuous change and revision of procedures and content to insure an informative, well-organized and worthwhile program.

School orientation must be of interest and value to the students. Following are some items which may be of benefit in planning such a program:

Orientation

I. Adjustment to Junior High/Middle School/High School
  A. Introduction of School Authorities and Personnel (Staff)
  B. The School Building Plan—locations of auditorium, cafeteria, school offices, rooms
  C. School Programs Offered: Academic, Social, Athletic, Health
  D. Rules and Regulation of the School
  E. Areas of Importance: Classwork, Discipline, Attendance
  F. How to Study—to work well, keep up and stay ahead
II. Student Government—Student Council, Student Congress

III. School History, Traditions, Mascot
IV. Curriculum and Other Services Offered
    A. Course offerings and requirements
    B. School Organizations
    C. Special Organizations, i.e., choirs
    D. Guidance Services
    E. Health Services
 V. Personal Development
    A. Personal appearance
    B. Developing personality
    C. Working to one's potential
    D. Setting high moral standards
    E. Learning to get along with others

Student Guidance Committees

A student guidance committee in cooperation with the guidance counselors may be formed. Regular members of a student guidance committee could be composed of students from the Student Council, Student Congress and representatives of the various grade levels in the school. Their work could be that of interpreting various areas of guidance services to the students, aiding in the setting up of a program for the year, assisting as aides in the counseling offices and carrying out various activities in the guidance program.

Student representatives provide a means of pupil involvement and of informing various school groups of the guidance activities. Other ways may be used involving the students in the program.

Student Newspapers and Yearbooks

Articles, pictures and notices of upcoming events concerning guidance could be included in both of these excellent public relations media—the student newspaper and the school yearbook.

Student Handbook

The guidance program and its available services could be included in a particular section of this handbook and given to students early in the year.

Student Council, Student Congress, or Student Government

Various members of the Student Council or Student Government may also be members of a student guidance committee and much information could be dispersed through this means.

Assembly Programs

Through skits, speeches and films, activities and services may be explained. Programs could be on student adjustment, moral values, student concerns, drugs, dropouts and career choices.

Bulletin Boards

Displays of charts, informative articles, bulletins and other pertinent information may be placed in classrooms, halls and offices.

Guidance Aides

Students may aid in passing out bulletins or performing other services in guidance during free periods. Such duties are not only for the better students but also for students who are in need of encouragement and recognition.

The above suggestions for use in enhancing the guidance program may not be of particular use in all areas of guidance work, but the thoughtful counselor may use those ideas that fit his particular group and school.

It is evident that many students, especially those who seldom visit the counselors have unclear images of the services offered and the views counselors hold of themselves and the services they offer. Many students feel that the only students who visit the counselors are those who have trouble with other students, teachers or with their classwork. Many teachers who themselves are hesitant in seeking the counselors' services cannot change these students' thinking a great deal. Even in schools with well-developed and sound guidance programs such views are held. Continuing an effective guidance program will enhance the counselor's program and his image.

Administration and the Board of Education

Responsibility for the development and administration of all aspects of communication with the public rests with the superintendent of schools. He should lead the board and staff to identify concerns on which communication efforts need to be focused. It is his responsibility to encourage principals, teachers and counselors to play their important roles in the large and continuous job of maintaining public understanding. The superintendent should mobilize the interests, efforts and loyalties of all who contribute to helping the community members understand the values and needs of a sound guidance program in the schools. It is necessary in theory and practice for the members of the school board to rely on the professionally trained superintendent for information and advice concerning the numerous technical concerns involved in and pertinent to the establishment of a good and helpful guidance program.

The symbol of educational leadership is the superintendent. When he exercises and exerts effective leadership, the symbol he embodies encourages public respect and also increases his capacity as a leader; when he fails to exhibit this leadership, respect for his office and his abilities declines and his capacity to influence public opinion and action is diminished. Principals are also educational leadership symbols, and although their functions differ from those of superintendents, they, too, share administrative responsibility for leadership and for keeping the public aware of what the schools are about.

The counselor in aiding in the establishment of a successful guidance program must keep the administration informed of problems and conditions requiring action.

Research has evidenced that people who are enthusiastic about their jobs and enjoy performing them are more productive and communicate more approval and goodwill. If staff members are displeased they work less effectively and complain often. Thus, high morale is a result of an effective and well-working guidance program.

Parents and Citizens

An essential part of public communications is maintaining good rapport and cooperative working relations with citizens in the community and parents who support the school and its guidance program. Parents discuss school at home with their children and with each other. They attend community organizations and school functions and discuss school with other citizens and parents in the community. Many community members and parents hold offices in school organizations, and many take an active part in various school activities where parents may be involved. Much of this informal participation is not a constant happening, but it serves to engender good working relationships between the parent and the school guidance program.

In most communities the Parent-Teacher Association has long played an important and uniquely constructive role in school and community relationships. This close association between parents and teachers gives the PTA intrinsic power which should include the guidance staff. Though PTA groups are not as strong as formerly, they continue to form a connecting link between the home and the school.

Many community leaders are members of social, civic, occupational, cultural, religious and fraternal groups which wield a great deal of influence on the actions and values in their communities. While the school is not the major concern of these organizations, when they are sufficiently motivated they are helpful in sponsoring scholarships, field trips, camps, career days, study groups, seminars, forums and other activities helpful to the schools and community members. Many business leaders, community workers and other leaders of these groups are happy to accommodate the schools in giving speeches, appearing on panels and contributing their services to school-related projects. If the public relations program is to be effective, persons other than members of the guidance staff must be called upon. Guidance workers can solicit the aid of individuals or groups in the guidance program, thereby enhancing the program and serving the needs of the school and the community's youth.

A Counselor's Self-Evaluation

The following Counselor's Self-Evaluation by this writer and a fellow counselor, James Cross, appeared at the end of the 1977 school year in the *Counselor's Mirror,* a publication of the Kansas City, Kansas, Public School District 500, Guidance and Personnel Services. It gives the guidance counselor an introspective look, a self-examination of his effectiveness throughout the year in his associations with his counselees:

> As the close of another school year approaches, it behooves each of us as counselors to take a good look at our performance over the year to see that we have measured up to the standards we feel an effective counselor must meet. In so doing, we are ascertaining whether or not we have functioned in a continuous process in assisting the students with whom we work to identify and meet their needs educationally, vocationally, socially and personally.
>
> Each of us should ask ourselves the following questions, then judge our performance accordingly:

- Have I aided in making pupil guidance services an integral and important phase of the total school program?
- Have I been a good listener and aided my counselees in arriving at intelligent decisions rather than being directive and impinging upon them my personal precepts?
- Have I aided students in their self-appraisal with intentions of helping them understand themselves, accept themselves and engender a firm desire to bring out the best in themselves?

- Have I studied each student carefully through varied records, tests, teacher and parent information and student, parent and teacher conferences to assess the student's interests, abilities and needs relative to his home, school and environment?
- Have I respected the integrity of my counselees, yet not foregoing actions conducive to their welfare and that of others who may be involved?
- Have I regarded each counselee as an individual and respected his right to acceptance as an important segment of society no matter what his status or problems?
- Have I maintained a professional attitude with students, yet made myself available and supportive when possible?
- Have I planned, researched, tested, evaluated and transmitted information which was beneficial in developing good habits and positive attitudes and values?
- Have I cooperated with administrators, teachers and parents and made referrals to the proper sources whenever my professional role limitations were inadequate or ineffective?
- Did I initiate a survey or projects during the school year that aided counselor services, improved counselor-student relationships and promoted improved relations with students, teachers and administrators?
- Finally, have I been helpful to students in understanding their strengths, weaknesses, interests, abilities and limitations, and in so doing have I helped them chart a course more effective for their own progress and benefit?

13

The Future of Education: Back to the Basics or a General Overhaul?

Twenty years ago, Robert Frost wrote that education is what you get if you hang around long enough. Without arguing with the poet, this report [A Nation at Risk] suggests that education is what we get if we commit enough time and people and money to our children. And if we don't, they may not have much more to do than hang around.

—James Wooten
ABC News Correspondent

The wisdom of Mr. Wooten's words are well spoken and their import should reach far and wide to everyone in our nation as we take stock of our public educational system. A new public awareness has come to the fore, an awareness that our educational system has come to a state of lethargy. Many of our children attend school only because it is mandatory up to a certain age, and some even escape that decree of compulsory education and, unable to find some type of job, resort to a haven at home doing nothing but watching television and having their parents have guilt feelings as they say to themselves: Where did I go wrong? Where did I fail? When some parents are asked whether or not they are encouraging their children to get in school and get moving—either in school or doing something constructive—the parents throw up their hands in desperation and say: "I've tried everything; I don't know what to do!"

Some students have little regard for learning, for low grades, for what the present will do in helping them to get ahead in the future. Many parents who are out working to barely feed and clothe their children, eking out a bare subsistence, are often too exhausted at the end of a busy day to realize when a report card has been issued, whether or not their children have homework to do or what their general progress in school is.

149

You may call it "laziness on the parents' part; that they just don't care," or whatever you like, but let's face it as it is. These parents are tired, they need the money to survive, so they must work; they must have money for bills, so they must work. With these things a reality, the job of the schools is even more significant than ever before, for it is at school and through associations with others that children receive an enthusiasm for learning, a zest for living and an incentive to make something of themselves.

Respect for one another, for those in authority, for adults in general and for life in particular has been so forgotten that security guards must patrol the halls all or a portion of the day in many schools throughout the nation to quell disruption from within and the unwarranted and un-solicited influx of influences from without.

Like a stinging blow to the face and a wide-eyed realization of the plight of education in the decade of the 80s comes the piercing report of the National Commission on Excellence in Education, *A Nation at Risk: The Imperative of Educational Reform.* The report's message is not glos-sed over or circuitous, but clear-cut and to the point: "We have in effect been committing an act of unthinking, unilateral educational disarma-ment." The commission's strident and scorching condemnation of educa-tion calls for the intensified action by national leaders and sounds an alarm and a directive to citizens to make provisions necessary for fiscal aid for educational reforms and teachers' salaries. "Our nation is at risk" because of a "rising tide of mediocrity in the classroom," reports the commission.

Another report causing our nation to scrutinize public education more closely is the College Board's report on the basic competencies that a good high school education should embody. Computer literacy in addition to education in the arts was stressed.

A report from the Task Force on Education for Economic Growth on the relationship between quality education and "our national survival" reiterates some of the recommendations set forth by *A Nation at Risk,* including more forceful federal leadership and increased teachers' salaries.

Adding to the impetus of public awareness of the schools' dilemmas is the *Twentieth Century Fund Report.* Calling for "a national commitment to excellence in our public schools," it is critical of any proposal to curtail public education funds.

Resulting from these reports, pressures at the national level and from the citizens in our nation, America's schools are reevaluating their credentials, searching their curriculums in a manner rivaling those made in 1957 following the launching of the Soviets' first spacecraft *Sputnik,* which was the stimulus to educational reform in America.

Numerous educational revisions and modifications are being made as the nation moves forward and assesses the road education must traverse or resist. In this last portion of the book, we will discuss some of the ideas for improvement and change that some authorities are stressing and the author's suggestions resulting from years of work in the field of education. Thus will be revealed what is being done to insure improvement in the outlook for students, teachers and the field of education and what is yet to be done.

It will be evidenced that educationists must reemphasize the basics, scrutinize existing programs and implement areas to reach a level of excellence in education in the 80s.

Raising the Status of Teachers

Improving the Teacher's Image through Salary, Exposure

While many Americans are summoning a return to the basics to improve our educational system, we must begin, first of all, with the human component through which education must be filtered and disseminated; the object of education's helpmate; the source of unlimited emulation—the teacher. The teacher is one of our nation's most valuable professionals, and an individual like Horace Mann so aptly stated that we need to find teachers who could "strike a victory for humanity," and we do have such teachers among us. A successful teacher possesses the skills of knowledge pertinent to the psychological principles of teaching, has competence in the liberal arts, particularly in the subject matter to be taught, as well as possessing a high degree of intelligence. The successful teacher is effective in the promotion of good working conditions with children, youth, young adults, parents, faculty members and administrative personnel. They must share in the leadership responsibilities in the school in addition to those they accept in their roles as teachers. In short, the teacher is the key to quality in education as he unlocks thousands upon thousands of doors to intellectual understanding.

If education is to be improved, the image and status of teachers, first of all, must be elevated and enhanced. They must be recognized as being important and offering service through which all individuals who become worthwhile in any endeavor in life, in any career, must of necessity need and accept.

Students are bypassing the teaching profession and finding employment in fields paying more money, affording more status and where they are appreciated for their contributions as individuals and, at the same time, can be void of the stress and strain often attendant with the school environment.

Television, radio, newspapers, motion pictures and other communication services need to promote, glamorize, enhance and elevate teaching to a highly respectable exposé like in soap operas, movies, cultural productions and exposure for recognition of outstanding contributions made by teachers and administrative personnel. They must show them as an example of beauty of spirit and appearance, with outgoing personalities, enthusiasm and dedication to their profession. Teachers could be elevated through the right commercials just as other professional groups are depicted. Only through proficient and superior teachers serving as role models for students can the teaching profession attract an intellectually high caliber of teachers to guide our children. Only would we buy inferior merchandise if we could do no better or were we unaware of its quality. Teachers need to be recognized, to be applauded and even lauded for their services. They should be called upon in the community to be ambassadors of goodwill and examples of community contributors of whom we are proud.

To recruit teachers, school boards must secure the services of competent individuals who will screen carefully all potential employees for their capabilities, school performance, appearance and ability to speak intelligently and to write in an acceptable manner. Many teachers are unable to communicate effectively with their students and parents; many are unable to put their thoughts into writing as well as the students they teach are able to do. Recruiters should be of different ethnic backgrounds, for only through understanding the culture of a people, their backgrounds and mores can a recruiter understand the rudiments and full import of what the ingredients of a good teacher are. A well-trained black is in a better position to hire a black teacher than is a white recruiter. A well-trained Hispanic recruiter could recognize some things in a prospective Hispanic or minority teacher than, perhaps, a recruiter of a race and background different from his own.

Patricia McCormack, UPI Education Editor, in a syndicated column wrote:

"Recent reports flunking the nation's schools have been laced with themes painting teachers as scapegoats, incompetents and worse.

"One wonders why anyone would study teaching or continue as a teacher—spitballs and all."

Patricia McCormack, in the same article, quotes some statements by Dr. Emily Freistritzer, a former teacher and publisher of two education newsletters, *Department of Education Weekly* and *Teacher Education Reports,* and the author of *The Condition of Teaching, a State-by-State Analysis,* published by the Carnegie Foundation for the Advancement of Teaching, Washington, D.C.

Dr. Freistritzer contends that teachers need to be placed on a pedestal as they once were.

"There needs to be rewards for excellence, as well as teacher appreciation movements," she stated.

"The teachers need to be looked up to in their communities and viewed as something special and respected," she said, then added, "Why can't a teacher be the speaker at the Rotary and Kiwanis Clubs, the Masons and all the rest?"

In the same article, Dr. Ernest L. Boyer, Carnegie Foundation president and former U.S. Commissioner of Education, agrees: "Teachers do not receive adequate recognition and reward."

A study of the American high school by the Carnegie Foundation has been completed, and Dr. Boyer felt his involvement in the project provided an opportunity for him to visit schools coast to coast. As a result, he made definite observations.

> Time and again, we were reminded that excellence in education means excellence in teaching, that improving schools means improving the working conditions of those who meet with students every day.
>
> We discovered in our study that teachers are troubled not only about salaries, but about loss of status, the bureaucratic pressure, a negative public image and the lack of recognition and rewards.

Dr. Freistritzer reiterated further that teachers choose teaching as a career for benefits beyond salary. Among these benefits are gaining satisfaction by helping someone, the joy of seeing a child's eyes light up, in addition to summer vacation and many school holidays.

Several remarkable statistics worthy of note were in her report: Of teachers' salaries, Alaska pays the most—$35,953—Mississippi the least—$14,285. Almost two-thirds of the states (31) pay below the national average—$20,531.

In some states salaries of teachers are given high priority. California, as a part of an education package totaling $800 million, is raising the base pay for teachers from an average of $13,500 to as much as $18,000 over a three-year period. California has begun a "mentor" program in which competent teachers will be paid $4,000 to help new teachers get off to a firm footing.

Some merit pay programs are being instituted in some states; for example, Florida has $50 million for discovering some plan for merit pay.

Merit pay seems questionable, for who is to determine criteria that would be reasonable in selecting those receiving such pay? Superintendents, principals, supervisors have little time for actual classroom visits enough times to assess fully teacher performance. Would a teacher's performance be determined by students' scores on specific national, state or local tests? Would tenure over the long haul be the answer? Would principal appraisal be the answer? Merit pay has been started in some districts but fizzled out because of the lack of fundamental definitives to abide by.

If the status of teachers is improved and the salaries are substantially enhanced, then the bright students should have enthusiasm for joining up with professionals in one of the most worthwhile professions in the world—that of teaching. The great pay is not in money but in the deepdown satisfaction that comes from nurturing great oaks from little acorns.

Thus it is incumbent upon each of us to change the results of the latest Gallup Poll on education which reveals the percentage of individuals who would want their children to become public school teachers hit its lowest point in fifteen years. In 1969, 75 percent of adults preferred their children to teach while only 45 percent shared this opinion in 1983.

In Kansas, education was the top priority at its 1984 January session of 165 legislative leaders in the state. John Carlin, governor of Kansas, and educational officials spurred on by many months of public clamor over the controversial *Nation at Risk* and by forums conducted across the state, moved into the 1984 session with both the intent and the dollars to place education as the mainstream of this year's legislative action. In addition to having a mandate from the public to address education, the legislature also has millions of dollars to use. These funds are the results of an improved economy and passage of the largest sales tax increase in the state's history.

Governor Carlin planned to submit an educational package with substantially higher teacher salaries as its main issue, a legislative education committee recommending merit pay, a teacher scholarship program and a slightly longer school year. The governor for the second year in a row recommended that before being certified by the state prospective teachers be given a special test. He also expressed the belief that strong support for testing future teachers would enable the public to know that increase in salaries would attract quality teachers.

Improving Discipline, a Major School Problem

According to the Gallup Poll on education, for the fourteenth time in fifteen years discipline ranks as the top problem in the nation's public schools. Of the 1,540 adults polled in the annual survey which appeared in the September issue of *Phi Delta Kappan* magazine, 25 percent of the persons surveyed listed lack of discipline as the leading problem. Seventy-two percent of those polled felt lack of discipline at home as the major cause, with 54 percent naming a lack of respect for law and authority and 42 percent placing the blame on teachers who are poorly trained (Phi Delta Kappan, September, 1983).

The Structure of School Improvement, a report by Richard H. Hersh, a dean of the graduate school, and his associates, Bruce R. Joyce and Michael McKibben, at the University of Oregon at Eugene, indicates that after going over twenty years of research they found certain characteristics always in evidence in the best schools. In addition to order and discipline included were: clear academic and behavioral goals for students, teachers who believe in their own talents, teachers and administrators who care about their students, more work time, frequent and monitored homework, an organized curriculum, variety of teaching strategies and opportunities for student responsibility.

Hersh and his associates believe that in the late 60s and early 70s was the time when order in the classroom got out of hand. He stated: "It was the students-know-best era."

Throughout the nation within the past decade, teachers have been stabbed, shot at, killed, maimed, verbally and physically abused, taken to court and their property harmed, to name a few of the indignities teachers have suffered. Many schools were forced to engage uniformed police officers to patrol the halls for school security, but most administrators felt this presented too severe a form of coercion. However, more stringent methods than teacher supervision needed to be instituted, thus in many schools across the nation security guards are on duty throughout the day and at many school activities held at night.

President Reagan recently voiced his determination to deal with discipline in American schools. Speaking before an administration-sponsored education summit at the National forum on Excellence in Education held in Indianapolis, the president called on the Justice Department to help restore discipline in America's schools, which he stated should be "temples of learning, not drug dens."

Although many attending educators were disturbed because he did not propose federal funds for schools, they applauded the president's concern for helping control discipline in the schools. Three million American high school students a month are victims. *Violence in Classrooms* was a special report presented to President Reagan and called for federal aid to help public schools impose stricter discipline.

The report, as a follow-up to the promise at the education forum in Indianapolis, *Chaos in the Classroom: Enemy of American Education,* was compiled by the president's Cabinet Council on Human Resources.

Consideration was given to how the Justice Department could aid in curbing vandalism and violence in public schools.

Alternative schools should be a part of every school system for those disruptive individuals who have not been helped through in-school suspension programs, whereby students must remain apart from other students yet carry on a well-structured program of education and adjustment. One or several of these alternative schools would serve an area or even a relatively small school district. The staff would consist of experts in the fields of education, psychology, guidance and social rehabilitation.

Discipline and the respect for oneself and the rights of others should begin early in the home where parents inculcate rules of behavior and the establishment of the meaning of right and wrong. Even if parents must be away at work, the children should be so instilled with these rules of behavior that they act properly when no adult is present. However, the best teaching in the world by the most well-meaning parents is no absolute guarantee that children's behavior will be above reproach.

In school, teachers must be kind but firm, have well-organized and challenging work planned, press for an environment conducive to learning and develop an enthusiasm that is contagious. The good teacher will establish very early a few simple and fair rules made with the students' help that they must learn to respect and follow. Students must understand that if rules are broken, they must suffer the consequences and be penalized when discovered. Above all, teachers must encourage students to respect themselves, their parents, teachers and other adults and their peers. When their own rights begin to infringe upon the rights of others, students must know it is then that their own rights end.

Parent involvement in PTA groups, school meetings, drug programs and group counseling sessions and making subject matter more meaningful and interesting can be some of the answers to the problems of discipline.

All teachers, particularly at the middle school level, may consult with one another to obtain information on the student's functioning characteristics, how they handled or were unable to cope with problems the student had in their classes. Collectively, in pooling their knowledge and exchanging techniques, ideas and skills, all of the teachers can help in the student's adjustment problems.

The counselor is in a positive position to know a great deal about a student. The counselor is able to look at the situation objectively, and if any of the contributing factors stem from the teacher, the counselor may offer suggestions; it is very important that the teacher be receptive to the counselor's suggestions for helping.

According to Stradley and Aspinall, in *Discipline in the Junior High/ Middle School: A Handbook for Teachers, Counselors and Administrators,* one of the most valuable documents a school can have is one related to an honor system.

The following code, called the Viking Pledge, was used in the authors' school. Developed by the students, the pledge is reviewed periodically by the Student Council:

> As a Viking:
> 1. I will treat others, classmates and staff members, as I would like them to treat me. To do this requires that I respect my teachers and fellow students, cooperate with them and hold my responsibilities to myself and to my school, seriously and with honor.
> 2. I will respect school property and the property of others without constant reminder. I will avoid defacing lockers, walls and desks. I will make neatness and cleanliness of the school building one of my individual responsibilities.
> 3. I will encourage courtesy and honor. I will develop character and maturity through acceptance of responsibility and self-control. I will make every effort to be prompt, dependable and trustworthy.
> 4. I will do the very best work of which I am capable to bring credit to myself, my home, my school and my community.
> 5. I will personally help to maintain law and order in the school and community. I will keep aware of all school regulations so that I may follow them with understanding.
> 6. I will try to grow away from immature habits, attitudes and approaches to my problems and make a strong attempt to act and seek solutions in a constructive manner as a responsible young adult.
> 7. I will accept correction and constructive criticism with a strong desire to improve myself.

Honor codes such as this should be developed by the students if they are to be meaningful. Student Councils, as in this particular school, reviewed the code yearly to ascertain a need for updating.

The honor code should be placed in conspicuous spots about the school that students may read it at their leisure. Call the code to the students' attention when they fail to follow the rules and keep before them that the code is to be respected and followed.

The following two memorandums may be discussed with middle school and high school students to help them understand that in order to succeed they must, first of all, learn to get along with people, accept responsibility and develop a pleasing personality. These were developed by and used by the author of this book.

To Students: Learn to Accept Responsibility

Students must learn to accept responsibility. Responsibility implies the act of being responsible; it is a care, a duty. It is the ability to fulfill one's obligations at home, at school, in the community or wherever you happen to be. It means doing those things expected of you as a family member, as a student, a citizen and as a member of any group to which you belong. To accept responsibility one is required to take charge of or be trusted with important matters, and in earning this trust you must be able to choose for yourself between right and wrong.

In order to accept responsibility and carry out required duties and obligations properly, an individual must develop a sense of respect, first of all for himself—and in so doing he will respect those in charge, whether they be adults or associates, at home, at school or in the community.

To develop self-respect, one must first begin with himself. Think highly of yourself. Realize that you are a person of value, one with something to offer—kindness to your friends and family, fairness in your dealings with others and an inner drive to make something of yourself and your life. Watch your actions, your language, your self-control at all times. Do those things that will enable you to respect yourself and will invite others to return that respect. Bad language and vulgar actions reveal not coyness or suaveness, but unadulterated, limited intelligence and crudeness.

You must learn to accept responsibility at home, at school and in the community. At home you must be a part of the family and accept the responsibility of performing your fair share of the work. Only through the cooperation of every member of your family can it be a happy one. Things will not always run smoothly, but they will more often if you do your part. Cultivate genuine love for people and that love will be returned. Do unto others as you would want others to do unto you.

At school there are certain rules and regulations that must be followed if progress is to be made. You are responsible for abiding by the rules and for holding yourself accountable for your own behavior. Rules are necessary because they insure a sensible way of getting things done. You must learn the rules and obey them if you want to get along well. Breaking the rules simply reveals childlike actions. Following the school's rules and regulations makes things easier for you because these rules were made with you in mind—to help you and to protect you.

Sensible and logical school rules have been set because of a need for them. They are to benefit a majority. Follow them and be a respected citizen. Accept, too, the responsibility of performing your work to the best of your ability. A responsible student controls himself in and out of the classroom, gives attention and participates in class, completing all assignments. If you are molding yourself into a worthwhile person, you can say that you are respectful of yourself and others, reliable, trustworthy and are able to choose between what is right and what is wrong. If you're in doubt about a thing you are about to do, weigh it first; there must be some doubt in your mind if you are hesitant. Failure to do those things expected of you is a reflection upon your parents. Are they the wrong type of parents? Respect them and honor them by your actions and deeds.

To Students: Develop Your Personality

Your personality is you, your whole self. It includes your physique or build, temperament, skills, interests, hopes, appearance, habits, intelligence, actions and achievements. It includes both what you are today and what you hope to be in the future. Personality includes how you relate (your feelings and reactions) to others and the experiences you encounter in doing so. Personality is subject, then, to the influence of the following main factors: (1) what you are born with (the way you look, your family and abilities); (2) your environment or surroundings (home, school, community) and (3) and the personal meanings and interpretations that you give to your experiences. Personality is what you mean when you refer to "I," or yourself. It is your total self composed of all the feelings, attitudes, values and behavior which make each person a unique individual. None of these things can be taken alone to determine your personality, but they all must be viewed as being related or working together to make you "you."

The things or aspects with which you are born or, as we say, you inherited include physique (build), physical appearance, the rate at which you mature and, to some extent, your ability to achieve. Our personalities, too, are influenced by our families, neighborhoods, community, school and the customs and the habits of the people with whom we live and associate.

In order to develop an acceptable personality each person must learn, first of all, to accept himself and to recognize his strengths and weaknesses. Accepting oneself is part of the process of growing up. Know that you are important. No one thing such as looks or ability determines your personality. In addition to looking at your experiences and your abilities and interests, you must consider what other people expect of you and you must accept this, also. Only until you accept yourself and know what is expected of you can you develop your personality to the extent that you can change some of the things about yourself that you want to change.

Every experience that you have, every activity that you engage in—all of your feelings, all of your ideas, your likes and dislikes, your abilities, the way you impress others, your actions and all of the special things about you—the way you talk, smile, all make up a distinct personality that is you.

A good personality, we can reasonably conclude, is one that is satisfying to the person himself and one which is satisfying and pleasing to others. To have a good or acceptably pleasing personality, one must be able to get along well with others, and he must have a variety of experiences and a variety of interests. A person with a well-rounded personality has enough worthwhile activities to keep himself stimulated so much that he is neither bored with himself nor with others. This, then, can be called a "healthy" personality. The person possessing a "healthy" personality likes himself and others and constantly looks for ways to improve himself and to help others. He is optimistic and looks on the bright side of life, changing the things that he can change that are undesirable and making the most of those about which he is able to do nothing.

14

The Need for More Precise Diagnostic Tools in Determining Student Deficiencies

Although numerous weekly or periodic teacher-made tests are directed toward the students and a multitude of standardized tests are prescribed by the central offices of a school district, there are yet no diagnostic instruments or measurements proficient enough to assess pupil growth. If such were available less time could be spent in teaching skills and attitudes that are unnecessary or already acquired.

There is no comprehensive measuring rod of student achievement. According to *New Trends in Education,* edited by William P. Lineberry: "Far more precise diagnostic tools are needed to pinpoint what is happening in the nation's schools, to show what children actually learn and when and how well they learn it."

Just how accurate standardized tests are as measurements of students' inherent intelligence or achievement is difficult to assess. Most average and below-average students and also some above average place little credence in serious performance on these tests. Many students guess, copy or mark hurriedly at random to get the job of testing over as quickly as possible. Very few students take the time, even when directed, to look over the test to check for accuracy. Test time is often only a routine activity and a chance to get out of class.

Today, more than ever before, the number of standardized tests students are taking is practically inestimable. Thousands of tests are available from job placement to any area of learning. Testing goes on from kindergarten throughout college. Even in preschool tools are used to gauge the abilities of the little ones. There are readiness tests to ascertain whether or not children are ready to read, "head" tests known as IQ tests attempt to discover how much ability is innate, inborn. Standardized tests are used in school subjects such as language arts, mathematics and science for comparison with other schools locally and nationwide, to discover student aptitude for various school subjects, their achievement from the onset of their education to their present level.

Resulting test scores are often the basis for a good or poor curriculum, measurement of a teacher's skill, the placement of students according to test scores and for a multitude of other yardsticks for appraising learning. Many educators and organizations are opposed to such standardized tests and attack them as being inaccurate instruments of evaluation. Some feel these tests are made for white middle class students, thus the terminology or language used in them lack relevancy and are not familiar to blacks, minorities and to the economically disadvantaged. The opposition feels that due to these inconsistencies, the tests are biased and inaccurate measurements.

Pressure is placed upon teachers to "teach the test," and failure to do so can result in poor teacher evaluations in performance and competency. The National Education Association and the National Association for the Advancement of Colored People, as well as other organizations, have questioned the validity of the tests and have called for their revision. Many of these groups believe inconsistencies and ambiguities exist, thus raising questions on their reliability and merit as a measurement of a student's abilities in various areas and his intelligence and achievement. Thus, these tests, some of which are outdated and some of which have been made easier in recent years for the students "to look better scorewise," are in need of close scrutiny by the test makers who must give credence to the needs of the students. Therefore, students as well as the teachers, should have some input into their content.

Because of the lack of precise diagnostic tools of measuring achievement, the Carnegie Corporation, in questioning the feasibility of a national assessment of education, organized a top level committee for this investigation. The committee concluded that such a project would be both feasible and desirable. Because of advances in the theory and technology of statistical sampling that random sample, according to Richard Scammon, a former director of the Bureau of the Census, of one-half of one percent of the population can provide data statistically accurate within a few percentage points.

Five percent of children in the nine-, thirteen- and seventeen-year age brackets and twenty-nine-year-old adults would be sampled by the Carnegie Committee. Those expected to have achieved the goals of the primary grades would be the nine-year-olds; elementary goals, thirteen-year-olds; and the seventeen-year-olds, secondary. The purpose for surveying the adults would be to compare them as representative of the educational level of the nation.

No identification of participating students, schools or teachers would be made. Breakdowns in such a study would be by sex, ethnicity, geographic region, socioeconomic level and by urban, suburban and rural areas. Assessment was planned to be every three or five years.

Only one student would be likely to be tested in a five-year period, taking only a small part of the entire test, which would take twenty hours for completion. The test would include seven subject areas: reading, language arts, mathematics, social studies, citizenship, fine arts and vocational education.

A consistent and comprehensive account of the accomplishments of the nation's educational system and pupil assessment could be made by tests such as these if applied nationwide.

The Armed Forces basic mental test, the AFQT (Armed Forces Qualification Test) and related tests are the best available indicator of state-by-state school performance and the closest measurement available to a national index of educational strengths and weaknesses.

The AFQT must be taken by all draftees and enlistees before entering any military branch of service. Administered on a uniform basis throughout the country, it is a standard examination. Designed and first used in 1950, the AFQT has undergone frequent revision. Four subject areas are covered in this test: vocabulary, arithmetic, spatial relationships and mechanical ability. Twenty-five questions are in each category and arranged in cycles of increasing difficulty in each of the test areas. Testing time is fifty minutes with emphasis on power rather than speed. While both education and intelligence affect the ability to score well, the Army contends that the AFQT is not an intelligence test nor a measure of educational attainment.

Data compiled from 1958 to 1965 reveal that men from the western and midwestern states consistently scored highest on the mental tests and those from the South consistently scored lowest. Why the differences? Are schools in some sections of the country better than others? Are certain sections of the country providing a better educational atmosphere than others? If so, why can't these areas be surveyed and the findings put to use in elevating all schools?

Cited by the National Commission on Excellence in Education (NCEE), the scores of approximately one million college-bound students taking the Scholastic Aptitude Test (SAT) declined annually for nineteen years before the 1982 leveling off period. The number of top students having a score of 650 or higher (out of a possible 800), on either section of the test, fell by 45 percent on the verbal section and by 23 percent on the math section between 1972 and 1982 (the number of students taking the test decreased by only 3 percent during that period).

The National Assessment of Educational Progress (NAEP) has conducted surveys over the past decade that reveal declines among high school students in math, science and writing abilities. It also revealed that students are failing to acquire so-called "higher" skills—how to evaluate and analyze information, to think critically and solve all but the most elementary mathematical problems.

Are we in need of comprehensive measuring rods and diagnostic techniques that we may know early those areas in need of press or revision? How are our schools stacking up? The time is now for assessing our educational needs for the new technological age requires sound, enlightened minds, critical thinking plus wise decision-making.

Developing More Accurate Prescriptions for Overcoming Educational Deficiencies

Many high school students entering colleges have discovered to their amazement that there are deficiencies in their educational record which prohibit them from being able to cope and adjust satisfactorily to course materials, particularly in English, literature, science, math, foreign languages and other subject areas. There is also a lack of learning for critical and analytical thinking and, as mentioned before in this book, the limitation of communication skills in the areas of speaking and writing. If a student is unable to communicate effectively, he is at a disadvantage in practically all subjects, for the ability to understand and apply materials in all subject matter is important in grasping a knowledge of that subject.

The Carnegie Foundation for the Advancement of Teachers issued a report recently that pointed out the need for reconstructing high schools to eliminate various limitations in the educational curriculum.

The study, *High Schools: A Report on Secondary Education in America,* written by Ernest L. Boyer, Carnegie president and a former commissioner of education, contrasts to the verdict reached in April, 1983, by the National Commission on Education decreeing the mediocrity of public education. The Carnegie study said: "Schools can rise no higher than the communities that support them. And to blame schools for the 'rising tide of mediocrity' is to confuse symptoms with the disease."

Three years and approximately $1 million were spent on the study. An educational panel of experts, prominent citizens and other teams of educators were sent to fifteen high schools for four-week visits. These teams were in contact with 16,000 public high schools attended by 3 million students.

Its findings included making languages top priority—the capacity to think critically and effectively through the written and spoken word. The study reported the mastery of English to be the first and most essential goal of education. Schools were urged to give English teachers time to critique student papers with no more than twenty students in each of two classes.

In most schools limiting English teachers to only two classes unless other classes in addition were given would hardly be feasible, but it is undeniably certain that not only in English, but also in other required classes as well as regular classes in elementary school, enrollments should be kept relatively small, for only when teachers can give more individual attention to students' needs for teaching, reteaching, examination of deficiencies and special help can academic improvement become visible.

More tutors are needed in the areas of English, reading and other required courses as well as in laboratories providing remedial assistance. With an overload of paperwork, teachers are in need of extra school time and helpers as paraprofessionals or aides. Presently, many dedicated teachers spend hours of their time away from school, checking tests, grading papers, deciphering teaching materials and making lesson plans. Very few other jobs require such special preparation away from the place of employment. The Carnegie study recommended giving teachers an hour of time daily for class-preparation and record-keeping; making regular teaching load four classes plus one period in small seminars or helping students on independent projects; and freeing teachers from such menial chores as monitoring halls and lunchrooms. Some schools have already placed some of these recommendations into practice. Teachers, however, need to be visible in halls or at their classroom doors in order to become known to students, to help students appreciate teacher concern and to keep hall disturbances to a minimum. Security guards cannot be accessible in every area of the school building.

The Carnegie study also advised the need for a core curriculum of required courses in literature, the arts, foreign language, history, civics, science, mathematics, technology and health for every student. Electives would be streamlined that two-thirds instead of half of the courses required for graduation would be mandatory.

Many schools are revamping their curriculum and increasing graduation requirements. While we are in accord with such alterations, there remains a need for administrators, teachers and students to all have some input in curriculum changes. Administrators and teaches are in pivotal positions to ascertain student needs.

Some students enroll in classes that are relatively easy and require little constructive thinking or effort in actual performance. Such "Mickey Mouse" courses add little or no knowledge to their field of learning.

America has long held a distinctive position in the areas of math and science; however, continued long-standing preeminence may be in jeopardy. Only one year of science and more than one year of high school math are required by only about one-third of the nation's school districts. Studies have shown that only half of all high school students take any math or science after the tenth grade. As a result, many of the more prestigious colleges have had to scrutinize their class offerings and reduce and alter them. Remedial math courses at the college level have escalated.

In Europe it is noted that all students are required to study and complete at least two foreign languages before graduating, and some countries require three in addition to English.

Some years ago a presidential commission discovered that among high school students only 15 percent study any foreign language. One reason was that only 8 percent of United States colleges required a foreign language for admission, from 34 percent a decade earlier. Some colleges in the past two decades eliminated foreign language requirements and offered electives in English and social studies, and many high schools followed suit.

The National Center for Education Statistics revealed that almost 33 percent of high school sophomores and 30 percent of seniors enrolled in remedial English and math in a recent school year.

The National Commission on Excellence in Education advocated that all students be required to take four years of English; three years each of science and social studies and one-half year of computer science. For college preparatory students, two years of foreign language should be required. These recommendations are valid, realistic and needed if our educational standards are to be improved.

In order to cope with these deficiencies some state boards of education and state educational agencies have increased graduation requirements. Some are requiring students in their senior year to take more academic courses rather than electives.

Local school districts throughout the United States are also implementing higher student standards. In the past several years approximately half of the high schools have increased their graduation requirements. About two-thirds of the high schools have instituted the requirement for the passing of competency testing as a requirement for high school graduation.

Colleges and universities have initiated tougher entrance examinations, causing high schools to rethink and revamp their own graduation requirements.

High school and college athletes must now prove their academic skills as well as their physical prowess. New rules for incoming students beginning in 1986 have been passed by the National Collegiate Athletic Association (NCAA), requiring students to attain minimum scores on college entrance tests and to have a C average in high school and to have in addition a C average in three years of English and two years of math courses.

Further means of eliminating student deficiencies would be to hire home-school coordinators who will help parents and students understand more clearly the school's objectives and, at the same time, encourage the student to stay on the track, which will eliminate failures and lead directly to the development of his capabilities. Some schools already employ home-school coordinators. Students then would be able to have some successes in school, for only through having even the smallest successes can they gain confidence in their own ability to grow and achieve. Any person or student, regardless of his background, his ethnicity, economic status or culture, must first in some way experience success in at least one important part of his life if he is to succeed. Failure in education at the elementary, middle school or junior high school, high school or college level reduces a student's chances for success in later life.

Dealing with Desegregation and Integration to Achieve Quality Education

Desegregation is an arrangement in which persons of different racial and ethnic backgrounds live, work, learn and interact in the same environment. By law desegregation is frequently attendant to court order and in the discontinuance of separation racially in public schools.

Since the 1954 decision abolishing segregation, schools across the nation have opened their doors to blacks who for long had been denied equal rights and equal opportunity. Persuasion and mandate by the federal government speeded up the desegregation process in many areas; however, total integration has not yet been accomplished. In cities where there are many school districts, it is in the center area where the concentration of blacks is found. Unless some arrangements are made with these surrounding districts, desegregation cannot be accomplished. Desegregation suits are now pending in Kansas City, Missouri, for this reason. Busing is the only answer to achieving integration of students in most inner cities because of totally segregated neighborhoods.

Many problems socially and educationally are involved in desegregation. Unless black students are average or above they are not encouraged generally, understood or given the push that is needed in making consistent progress. In the case of many minorities, their socioeconomic level, unstable families, one-parent families, community attitudes and often low educational level of parents place minority students at a disadvantage in verbal skills which the schools have not alleviated nor tried with much effort to erase. While blacks score below whites on some tests, many blacks outperform whites, and in some geographic areas in the South blacks often score lower than those in the North.

More money for specialists, tutors, quality teachers and surveys to help these students reach their potentialities are expedient. Specialization is so evident in help for children with special physical and social problems that teachers must constantly dismiss sudents throughout the day. More laboratories, tutors and special classes could be incorporated. Although there are schools in disadvantaged areas or schools having students from disadvantaged areas which have government-funded labs for reading and math, many students in need of these services cannot obtain the services because of limited space to accommodate them.

Longer School Hours: Is This the Answer?

With the many criticisms of education coming from all fronts leveling cries of mediocrity in education, it is little wonder that educational groups and special commissions are taking the lead in attempting to discover the reasons for the backward plummeting of our children educationally.

Some feel that longer school days and a longer school year are the answer to the improvement of our educational system. Many groups and authorities have questioned whether or not this would actually upgrade education. Serious consideration has been given to extending the school day and year as has been done in Florida and California. Advocates of the extension cite the 240-day year in Japan in comparison to the 180-day year in the United States. In other countries the average regular school day is six to eight hours long in comparison to our six-hour day. A seven-hour school day and a 200- to 220-day school year have been recommended by the National Commission on Excellence in Education.

Teachers who enjoy the benefits of a lengthened vacation and a day with some periods free for planning are not in accord with the NCEE's proposal. In a survey taken by the Kansas National Education Association (KNEA) only 14 percent of the teachers endorsed the recommendation that the school day and year be lengthened and 69 percent opposed.

In the Kansas Association of School Boards' survey, a minority, only 32 percent, favored such a proposal. John Lloyd, KNEA executive director, indicated that teachers already work an average of sixty-three hours a week during the school year and are in need of the three-month breaks they get in the summer. He feels that teachers want to examine the quality of education, rather than the quantity.

Recently two school districts in north Carolina added twenty days to their school year. In New York, the Board of Regents has proposed adding time, and school officials in Illinois and Ohio are expected to do the same. Lengthening school days, whether students would profit educationally, would remove some part-time teenagers from the job market and would keep students off the streets for a longer period of time. Many working parents and single-parent families are concerned about their children's whereabouts in the evening. In many school districts schools are not dismissed early unless parents have been notified beforehand to make provisions for their children's care.

Lengthening the school day and year would increase the school budget to a significant degree, and only if school authorities, teachers and parents became sufficiently dedicated to help in upgrading the schools would the end justify the means. If students and teachers are to be clock-watchers and mark time until dismissal, it is questionable that a change would be warranted.

School Dropouts: What Can Be Done?

In the typical American high school, whether it is large and comprehensive or small and rural in its setting, it is estimated that half of the adolescents will quit school before receiving a diploma, and this half will come mainly from the lower classes. Many of those who leave school will have associations with those who remain. Many of the upper-class and some of the upper-middle-class children will be sent to private schools while many of the Catholics attend parochial schools. It is felt by some authorities that there exists in many high schools separation within public schools according to the curriculum, as in one high school there are four distinct courses of study: college preparatory, commercial, general and trade. There seems to be a distinct correlation between prestige class and curriculum choices with this separation, and this separation seems to be carried over into cliques within the school.

The social minority of today is the high school dropout. What type of employment is available to him? In the machine-oriented society with its computers and key-punching jobs, he has little opportunity to bargain for a job or to expand himself in this new society. The proportion of youth out of school and out of work exceeds the number in the depression of the 30s. Many dropouts no longer look for work anymore and therefore are not listed among the unemployed. From this hard core of dropouts come some of the hoodlums, drug addicts, gangsters, irresponsible and illegitimate parents who depend upon society for their subsistence.

Four out of five dropouts are white, though the dropout rate among blacks is twice as high as it is among whites. The greater percentage of dropouts originate in the blue and lower white collar socioeconomic classes, though the dropout groups includes all ethnic, geographic bounds and social classes. Some 15 percent of the total dropouts, according to some authorities, would have sufficient ability to finish high school; many have IQs between 75 and 90, but, as a general rule, individuals with such IQs complete high school. Lost through dropping out of the secondary schools is 25 percent of the country's top talent. Thus, it is noted that the dropout rate is not only in the sphere of the intellectually low, but includes some of the intellectually valuable students who could be contributing members to society.

It is estimated that most dropouts withdraw from school on or before age sixteen. This is the compulsory school age in many school districts. Nationally the dropout rate is higher in the South than in the North and higher among boys than girls; higher in the slums than in the suburbs. The delinquency rate is ten times as high among dropouts as among those students who remain in school.

Teachers and parents must be aware of some of the characteristics of potential dropouts in order to avert or redirect their direction for good if possible. These characteristics pertain to school, family and peers. In school these students are unable to read accurately and to communicate freely; they are generally noted to be behind in both reading and mathematics at the seventh-grade level while the majority of their grades are below standard for their grade level.

These dropouts have, as a rule, not moved through school without interruption. They have usually failed in one or more school years (first, second, eighth, ninth), most commonly failed; 85 percent of dropouts were behind one year; 53 percent two or more years. Attendance for these students is obviously irregular with attendant tardies and various illnesses given as reasons. Their performance is usually below their capabilities and no participation in extracurricular activities is evidenced. Many change schools frequently and are involved in trouble of various types and problems requiring disciplinary measures. Attitudinal, social and physical reasons are characteristics of actual or potential dropouts as not being accepted or "belonging" because of personality, nationality, family standing, size, speech, dress, lack of friends among students or teaching staff.

In the family certain characteristics are also found. Often there are more children than parents are able to control, such as an only child for a divorced or working mother; with five or more children for nondivorced and working mother of blue and lower white-collar class. Parents of these dropouts are often inconsistent in showing affection and in disciplining in addition to fostering unhappy family situations in which acceptance and easy communications are not apparent. The education level of parents of these children is the eighth grade, and the father figure is either weak or absent. There are few family friends among whom have problems of delinquency, desertion and divorce within the family unit.

Most dropouts have similar characteristics in dealing with their associates or peers. Their friends are not usually acceptable to their parents, are older or younger and not school oriented. These students possess a weak self-image and resent authority in almost all areas. Thus, many dropouts are poorly equipped intellectually, lack interest in school because of their inability to achieve, have little encouragement from home, school and friends, lack confidence in themselves and in their ability to reach goals. Some lack the necessary funds for ordinary needs and feel that they can earn a reasonable living with what they already know.

It is highly important that well-qualified and highly motivated teachers are hired and are given small classes that they may give more individual attention, encouragement and help to students. Counseling is needed early even from the beginning years of elementary school and before. Beginning guidance in the middle school or junior high school is too late for the potential dropout. Authorities believe the fifth grade is the latest that counseling services can reasonably be introduced to the potential dropout. Through the use of tests, measuring techniques and interviews, the counselor may place a slow or disadvantaged student in a special class for special or remedial services. Counseling services should be available to the total community as well as to the schools. A ratio of 1 counselor to 600 pupils in a middle class neighborhood and 1 to 300 in lower socioeconomic levels seems practical. School guidance services should be available to all students. Emphasis should be placed on how to secure a job, human relations and the importance of choosing proper courses in school.

A community body of representatives, community at large, the schools, churches, social agencies, business groups, labor groups, clubs, social organizations and government agencies could be established to implement programs, jobs, counseling services and skill centers for potential and actual dropouts.

The Need in Teacher Education—
Educationists Think It Is in Need of Upgrading

Our American public has placed a high value on education, for it is to the educators that they offer their children to be educated for their children's own productive ends and good and for the ultimate strength of the nation. We believe most citizens have left the quality of teaching in elementary and secondary schools to boards of education, both state and local, to make the final decisions as to the teachers' desirability and qualifications for the job. To attract individuals into the field of education, the field of teacher education must be upgraded and made more attractive and acceptable to students of high capabilities.

Though there is a fundamental conservatism in education and criticism is not always readily acceptable or amenable to change by those professionals steeped in traditional theories, in spite of these diehards evidences are prevalent that changes are being brought about. The problem of attracting persons of high ability to the teaching profession and the also difficult task of giving them an education befitting a high-caliber teacher are no easy responsibilities.

We already have among us teachers of excellent ability, dedication and sincere commitment without regard to pay commensurate with their services and abilities. Authorities continue to contend that the basic problem is that there. are not enough of these teachers in acceptable numbers. The character and quality of teacher education is being evaluated in our schools of education and colleges. While facilities, salaries, equipment and administration are important and must be reckoned with, we must realize that the quality of the education in this country can be no better than the intellectual level of its teachers and the high type of relevant. educational institutions in which they are trained. It is reasonable to believe that offering teacher scholarships, establishing future teacher programs in the secondary schools, stiffening demands made upon students entering the field and tightening requirements for admission to teaching programs will attract more top students to the teaching profession. As it is now, top students are being lost to business, science and more lucrative fields that are more satisfying financially and socially.

Teachers in all areas of the profession must have a certain number of hours in Education (the word Education is herein capitalized to denote the area of Teacher Education) and certain courses if they are to become certified in their state to participate in the teaching profession. Professional Education in which potential and practicing teachers are involved is the largest single field in higher education. Approximately one-third of all bachelor's degrees awarded in the past decade by United States schools of higher education were awarded in Education. About one-half of all master's degrees awarded each year are in this field, and it produces more doctorates (1,500 to 2,000 a year) than any other one field. Teacher training programs and other professional Education program areas are found in 80 percent of all accredited universities and colleges. Over 20,000 faculty members are employed full-time, which is more than in any other field of higher education with the exception of English. The network of professional structures surrounding the training programs encompass numerous professional state and national organizations of prestige, influence and of financial value.

The powerful National Education Association and its many departments, commissions and state and local affiliates are constantly touting the battle for the rights and humane treatment of teachers and their welfare in every conceivable manner. Numerous changes, reforms, concessions and teacher rights and privileges have come about because of its dynamic and forceful intercession and closely knit organization. Thousands of teachers agree on its benefits of membership. Other institutions like the United States Office of Education; state Departments of Education; national, state and local accrediting agencies and many other educational organizations and associations form a hierarchy of supporting institutions for the operation and promotion of the field of Education. One author contends that the size of Education has reached such a proportion and diversity that 95 percent of its time is spent in supplying the teaching market rather than upgrading the profession through important research, improving teacher education programs and raising its standard generally.

After practically a century of developing Education programs, many educators are yet uncertain of what Education is supposed to do. The fathers of Education who brought the study of Education to American colleges and universities during the last quarter of the nineteenth century possessed only vague ideas of the direction it would take and the nature of its development. These developers realized a need for a discipline for working with escalating enrollments in institutions of higher education and the structured pedagogy from Europe.

The one- and two-year teacher-training programs of the normal schools were felt by the early educators to be unable to contend with the mounting developmental problems of education. Normal schools, which were teaching preparatory schools, began in the 1820s as private schools but were soon followed by public institutions. Thus, the only formal instruction in pedagogy or teaching was given in the United States by these schools until the 1870s and 1880s when centers of learning such as the State University of Iowa, Johns Hopkins, Teachers College (Columbia University) and the University of Michigan began the institute course work in Education. The normal school for almost a century was not a part of higher education, but was somewhat of a technical school between the public schools and the colleges. The normal schools often took students who had no high school work and under a staff of former school teachers trained them for the elementary schools. High school students in the twentieth century were trained in the normal schools which became teachers colleges or four-year institutions and began to train students for the high schools. Since these beginnings, educators are continuing to clarify and identify skills, attitudes and the like as to their importance in Teacher Education. Educationists in various studies such as the ones made in the 60s by the Fund for the Advancement of Education have made significant findings. Among them are the irrelevancy of many college courses teaching candidates must take; that many teacher education programs are deficient to the extent that they actually confuse beginning teachers who attempt to put into practice what they have been taught.

Other educationists agree on a need for a more flexible system to substitute for the present rigid method of state certification with its mandated courses; and some also have suggested a need for a fifth year of preparation for teachers, and the direction of professional work in teacher education must be toward more rigorous, disciplined, relevant and more scholarly training. Others believe that the preparation for teaching may take forms not restricted to formal courses and to practice or student teaching. This intellectual exploration and inquiry could be in the form of independent study, seminars and internships.

Educationists also feel that the textbooks in Education should be reexamined. Some, they feel, are by relatively little-known writers who are not authorities in the field; that they are of low intellectual level, are large, heavy and expensive, evidence duplication of material and ideas from course to course. Like anything material in life, a general overhaul may be needed at times to sort out or refurbish the useful and discard the useless. The teaching of these Education courses are in need of revitalizing and being made more relevant to the needs of those to be served by the prospective teachers. Do we need beginning teachers to have a year of training within the school with a supervisor in charge?

Let all media of communication focus on the teachers in all their glory, for it is through teaching that all avocations had their beginning and their development.

Grading: Is Our System Adequate? Does It Need Changing?

Some educationists advocate schools without grades, ungraded classes where students move through school at their own rate. These schools practicing such educational innovations have had gratifying results with resultant high test scores. The students are neither promoted nor failed and receive no report cards. Their toughest competition is to achieve to the limit of their own capabilities. Such is the Continuous Progress Plan in the elementary schools of Appleton, Wisconsin, in which school authorities feel their program lends itself to the recognition of individual differences. Children enter a three-year program in elementary school. No grade labels are given but students are expected to complete successfully a stringent academic three-year bloc. Two conferences are held with parents, who are told of their child's strengths and weaknesses, and a progress report is given at mid-year. No lists, marks or characteristics are indicated, but the report indicates with clarity and preciseness the child's performance in relation to his abilities.

This three-year period is followed by three years of intermediate school. Achievement tests enable teachers to identify accomplishments and failings at parent-teacher conferences. The student participates in the conferences during the final year of intermediate school. Following this six-year period, most children enter junior high school; however, those who exhibit immaturity or academic weaknesses may remain a year, but such decisions have been made earlier in the year with the parents' knowledge in order that the retention will be agreeable with the parents and less traumatic for the child. Under the Continuous Progress Plan very few students remain, less than one-half of one percent.

Progress reports seem logical in the lower grades, and the theory of individual differences can be recognized more effectively. Children are not crushed by low marks, and parents are more involved in their children's continuous development. However, on the secondary level, grades seem to be an incentive for the average and the above-average students to strive harder in reaching their goals. Deficiency reports or down slips are used in many schools to inform the parents early in the grading period that their child is deficient in some area. Probable reasons for these deficiencies are given. Such reports are useful in helping parents encourage their children and in aiding students in noting where they stand in their classwork.

There are students each year who need to attend summer school. They desire to make up requirements, to take classes over that they have failed, or to get ahead in their classwork to make room for other courses during the regular school term. Some districts maintain summer schools; others do not. Some fail to have them because of lack of funds, too few participants and lack of transportation to the site of the classes. Because many of the students in need of these services are bused during the regular year, they cannot attend classes because of this lack and others cannot afford the tuition though it is usually minimal. These schools should be revived even if it means providing transportation, giving scholarships to deserving students who are disadvantaged and giving other students the opportunity to start the following school year with a cleaner slate.

Homework: How Much Is Too Much?

Parents throughout the nation are complaining constantly that their children have no homework or very little. They feel if their children had more homework they would learn more and consequently would make better marks in school. For many years in most secondary schools homework assignments have been started in class before the period was over. Should questions on exactly what was to be done or if directions were in need of clarification, the teacher was present to help. Unless the assignment called for a special report, more than half of the class assignment could be completed before the end of the period. For above-average students, many assignments are completed before a student leaves class.

Assignments may be in the form of books to be read or reviewed or the study of several chapters. If students have well-planned assignments that are not too lengthy and that they can understand, then such assignments are of value. However, often when teachers are upset with students or to fulfill parent expectations, they give lengthy and irrelevant assignments. Many times students have several classes in which excessive assignments are given. The conscientious students often labor long into the night while the less conscientious and slower students fail to try.

If homework is given it should be checked, but with teachers already overtaxed it is difficult to perform a thorough job of checking at all times. Young students need homework for the practice and reinforcement of skills such as reviewing spelling words and arithmetic tables. They do not need assignments that parents complete or through which parents attempt to show the teacher how much their child knows.

A special place in the home should be provided for study, but many students who fail to work too well under the best circumstances find it difficult to study with five or six family members talking and playing and the television blasting. As a result, there is no conceivable way that much work can be accomplished.

No matter how superior a teacher may be, he rarely, if ever, will have 100 percent of the students bring in home assignments. The nearest to acquiring such a state would be to give special credit for such assignments or some type of credit. School, adolescence relevant to this period and homework all combine to bring about serious tensions and ill feelings between parents and young people.

All teachers must think through their assignments, explain them thoroughly again and again if they seem nebulous and exclude all material that is not relevant to the work being studied. Work that the teacher will not have time to check or the class or paraprofessionals cannot check should also be excluded.

The National Commission on Excellence in Education reported that two-thirds of high school seniors now spend less than one hour a night on homework. The commission advocated that: "Students in high school should be assigned far more homework than now is the case."

This contention is to be considered, but time should be given in class to work on assignments, and such assignments must be checked if their use is to be justified and if they are to serve the purpose of increasing the students' growth.

Religion: Will It Help in Education?

According to a 1983 Gallup poll, most Americans are more interested today in religion than they were five years ago. This poll, however, reveals that fewer than half said that they participate in activities of a religious nature.

Pollster George Gallup stated: "Religious interest and involvement are extremely high in this country and growing, but deep commitment levels are still at a fairly low level."

When persons polled were asked if they were more likely today than five years ago to believe that religion could answer the problems of the world, 54 percent answered yes and 26 percent said no. Of those polled 85 percent said they thought it was important for Americans to become more interested in religion.

When young students are asked if they attend Sunday school and church most reply no and add that on Sundays they sleep late, then watch television.

Without the Lord's Prayer a part of the public schools, religion has no noticeable significance in public education. In families where strong religious ties exist, the institution of marriage is more meaningful and the children in these homes are mannerly, unselfish and caring. They have inner calmness and peace that tend to radiate about their countenances. A belief in God and the practice of the tenets of salvation give direction to children's lives and characters to their being. By studying the lives and ways of biblical characters and the exemplary life of Jesus Christ they are able to add depth and meaning to their existence.

A study which concentrated on the relationship existing between adult religious behavior and Catholic education was the Greeley-Rossi study. The study revealed that the relation between the religious education given in a Catholic school and adult behavior is noticeably stronger in those persons reared in devout families. Thus, they believed classroom religious education is more effective if it is reinforced by parent example.

Most churches today have a bus ministry since churches are often long distances from members' homes and transportation facilities are often ineffective. Buses transport many children and adults to and from worship services in churches of numerous denominations. Attending worship service is one of the best methods of inculcating habits of honest and clean living even though often many young churchgoers stray from the flock.

Conclusion

The author's intention has been to give officials, administrators, school personnel, the public and young adults a look back in education, a critical view of the present and a projection for the future. Concern for educational advancement has been minimal for the monumental problems obviously facing our schools and the slow growth of the students. The problems are too large to be dealt with without federal concern and funding.

The caliber of teachers must be improved and teacher standards upgraded. While we expect nothing short of the best from our children, we should accept nothing but the best from the teachers. To insure the improvement of teachers and to attract top students to the profession, improved monetary compensation must be forthcoming. The public must demand student reform and improvement. Teachers must not be looked upon as paid baby-sitters and students must wake up to the realization that they'll get out of learning what they put into it.

With modern scientific knowledge and the need for skill training, students must be constantly reminded that the lethargic ones among them will be unable to maintain the pace of this fast-moving society. Those who are indifferent and apathetic will only join the ranks of the poor and the jobless. Student standards, requirements and expectations must be accelerated.

Education is a right of all Americans and it is society's obligation to demand that each child be helped to reach his potential through concern, taxation and involvement. Whites and minorities must cooperate and progress amicably if this nation is to advance. The job market must be lucid and open to all nationalities, and students must be trained for jobs no less commensurate with their abilities. It is imperative and obligatory that educators continue to be vigilant, to research the discipline and make recommendations for upgrading all areas of the field. Ways must be discovered to increase interest and enthusiasm in material being taught and to develop a desire in students to want to learn and to explore. There is also a need to engender attitudes and values concerning intellectual activity that students can understand.

In short, we must develop a sensitivity not only to the practicality of education, but also to its relevance in today's living—to its quality and content. Our new age of technology of computerization, automation, space exploration and control systems has increased an interest in what our young people are learning. There is no room for apathetic hesitation, because it will be the eventual decisions and actions by young people that our nation will persevere and remain secure for generations of children to come.

Bacon, Margaret and Jones, Mary Brush. *Teen-Age Drinking.* Thomas Y. Crowell Co., N.Y., 1968.

Boyd, William and King, Edmund J. *The History of Western Education,* 8th ed., 1966.

Boyer, James B. and Joe L. *Curriculum & Instruction after Desegregation: Form, Substance and Proposals.* A. G. Press paperback, Manhattan, Kansas, 1975.

Brown, William E. and Greeley, Andrew N. *Can Catholic Schools Survive?* Sheed and Ward, N.Y., 1970.

Cervantes, Lucius F. *The Dropouts, Causes & Cures.* University of Michigan Press, Ann Arbor, 1965.

Cross, Wilbur. *Kids and Booze, What You Must Know to Help Them.* E. P. Dutton, N.Y., 1979.

Crow, Alice and Lester D. *An Introduction to Guidance.* American Book Company, N.Y., 1951.

————. *Organization and Conduct of Guidance Services.* David McKay Company, Inc., N.Y., 1965.

Experimental Designs Committee of the Association for Counselor Education and Supervision. *Research Guidelines for High School Counselors.* College Entrance Examination Board, N.Y., 1967.

Fulfilling the Letter and Spirit of the Law, Desegregation of the Nation's Schools—A Report of the United States Commission on Civil Rights, August. 1976.

Glasser, William, M.D. *Schools Without Failure.* Harper and Row, N.Y., 1969.

Good, Harry G. and Teller, James D. *A History of Western Education,* 3rd ed., 1969.

181

Griffin, Mary, M.D. and Felsenthal, Carole. *A Cry for Help.* Doubleday & Co., Inc., N.Y., 1983.

Henry, Nelson B. *Personnel Services in Education.* McKnight and McKnight, Illinois, 1947.

Hicks, William V. and Jameson, Marshall C. *The Elementary School Principal at Work.* Prentice-Hall, Inc., Englewood Cliffs, N.J., 1957.

Hollis, Joseph and Hollis, Lucille. *Organization for Effective Guidance.* Science Research Associates, Inc., Chicago, 1965.

Jencks. *A Reassessment of the Effect of Family and Schooling in America.* Basic Books, Inc., N.Y., 1972.

Koerner, James D. *The Miseducation of American Teachers.* Houghton & Mifflin Co., The Riverside Press, Cambridge, 1963.

Koob, Albert and Shaw, Russell. *S.O.S. for Catholic Schools.* Holt, Rinehart and Winston, N.Y., 1970.

Levine, Daniel U. and Havighurst, Robert J., editors. *Farewell to Schools???* Charles A. Jones Publishing Co., Worthington, Ohio, 1971.

Lichter, Solomon O., Rapien, Elsie B., Seibert, Frances M., Sklansky, Morris A., M.D. *The Drop-Outs.* Free Press of Glencoe, N.Y., 1962

Lineberry, William P. *New Trends in the Schools.* H. W. Wilson Co., N.Y., 1967.

Lloyd, Donald and Warfel, Harry R. *American English in Its Cultural Setting.* Alfred Knopf, N.Y., 1956.

Lokos, Lionel. *The Life and Legacy of Martin Luther King, House Divided.* Arlington House, New Rochelle, N.Y., 1968.

Mann, Peggy. *Ralph Bunche, U.N. Peacemaker.* Coward, McCann & Georghegan, Inc., N.Y. 1975.

Mathewson, Robert. *Guidance Policy and Practice.* Harper & Row, N.Y., 1962.

Mead, *Coming of Age in Samoa.* Dell Publishing Co., Third Laurel Printing, Dell Publishing Co., Inc., 1970.

Moses, Donald A. and Burger, Robert E. *Are You Driving Your Children to Drink?* Litton Educational Publishing, Inc., 1975.

NEA Research Bulletin, Vol. 44. Research Division, National Education Association, 1966.

Parker, Don H. *Schooling for What? Sex, Money, War, Peace.* McGraw-Hill Book Co., N.Y., 1970.

Sanders, David C., NEA and the Department of Elementary School Principals. *Elementary Education and the Academically Talented Pupil.* National Education Association, 1961.

Smith, Kenneth L. and Zepp, Jr., Ira G. *Search for the Beloved Community: The Thinking of Martin Luther King, Jr.* Judson Press, Valley Forge, 1972.

Stradley, William E. and Aspinall, Richard D. *Discipline in the Junior High, Middle School: A Handbook for Teachers, Counselors and Administrators.* The Center for Applied Research in Education, Inc., N.Y., 1975.

St. John, Nancy H. *School Desegregation,* John Wiley & Sons, N.Y., 1975.

Super, Donald E. *Charting Our Fields* (1948).

Wilkinson, J. Harvey III. *From Brown to Bakke, The Supreme Court and School Integration: 1954–1978.* Oxford University Press, 1979.

Williams, Gertrude J. and Money, John. *Traumatic Abuse and Neglect of Children at Home.* Johns Hopkins University Press, Baltimore, Maryland, 1980.